THE
MISSING
ONES

A True Story

By

Dan Pontbriand

Order this book on line at www.amazon.com

Printed in the United States of America.

ISBN-13: 978-1490434049

ISBN-10: 1490434046

Library of Congress Control Number: 2014906524

First Edition – 08/17/2012

Second Edition – 04/15/2014

THIS BOOK IS DEDICTED TO

BOB CASO

WHO NEVER GAVE UP SEARCHING

CONTENTS

FORWARD

Two thousand and one was a momentous year. When I look back at it, my thoughts are often dominated by the horrors of September 11. For me and other members of a very unique team however, it was also the beginning of a very positive period of keen adventure, searching and mystery. As the world seemed to be pulling itself apart elsewhere, in an isolated section of the Pacific Northwest, we somehow managed to become part of an effort to solve a missing-persons case that had haunted a family for well over seventy years. Our adventure went on for three years and ultimately ended in success. During that time, each of us kindled friendships that would last a lifetime.

As you read through the following pages, you will become acquainted with members of our team and the purposes that drove each of us. Specifically, you will gain a strong sense of two particular men; people who really mattered.

Dan Pontbriand, the author of this book, was our team leader. I respect him enormously. Dan is organized and thorough, and when engaged in something important, he is incredibly driven. As such, he was the perfect leader for a team of independent divers and explorers use to having things their own way. Once introduced to the Warren mystery by Bob Caso, Dan launched a completely new investigation using modern techniques and equipment that led to the solving of the mystery.

Bob Caso, a veteran diver from the 1950s, was quite literally the "historian" for the missing members of the Warren family. Bob's devotion to their memory was the primary factor that started our "modern" search. Without his involvement and interest in the case that spanned decades, none of us would have even known about the missing couple, let alone be involved in a dynamic search to solve the mystery of their disappearance.

Without these two men, quite literally none of what you are about to read regarding this modern search would have ever happened. Together, they made a real difference, and our team was successful as a result. I'm proud to call each of them my friend. I hope that you will enjoy reading about this thrilling search as much as I did while leafing through the pages and reminiscing about it. It's an extremely fine thing to be able to look back and realize that we were all part of something that truly mattered.

John Rawlings
Mill Creek, Washington
June, 2012

ACKNOWLEDGEMENTS

Special Thanks

Contributors:

Aberdeen Daily World
Kristin Dizon Andersen, Seattle Post-Intelligencer
Lake Crescent Lodge
Log Cabin Resort
Kathy Monds, Clallam Historical Society
Peninsula Daily News
Peninsula News Network
Peninsula Television Network
Sol Duc Resort

The Family:

Louise Alton Allen
Phoebe Warren Bardin
Nicholas Warren Coachman
Mary Lou Rhone Elwood
Jessie Wilma Matteson Ewing
Kristine Warren Grube
Ann Klein
Patty Warren Smith
James Warren
Roland and Geneil Warren

Good Friends:

Robert "Bob" Caso
Justine Chorley
Ed and Dale Jacobs
Beverly Sherman
Dale and Dee Dee Steele

The Team:

Laurie Axelson – NPS-Olympic NP
Jim Bradford – NPS-SCR
Phil Breed
Dr. Dave Conlin – NPS-SRC
Greg Gambill
Mike Kalahar – NPS – Olympic NP
Dan Lenihan - NPS-SRC (retired)
Tony Lutz – NPS-Olympic NP
Dan Messaros – NPS – Olympic NP
Larry Murphy – NPS-SRC
John Rawlings
Lynn Roberson – NPS-Olympic NP
Gene and Sandra Ralston
Jerome Ryan
Art Sandison – NPS-Olympic NP
Paul Seylor – NPS- Olympic NP
Brett Seymour – NPS-SRC
Victoria Sonne – NPS-Olympic NP
Carl Stieglitz
Aaron Titus – NPS–Olympic NP
Bill Walker
Joe Walker
Dan Warter
Randy Williams

Olympic National Park Personnel:

Ed Books - Lake Crescent Maintenance
David Conca - Cultural Resource Specialist
Dr. Paul Gleeson - Chief of Cultural Resources (retired)
Kevin Hendricks – Assistant Chief Ranger
Barb Maynes - Public Information Officer
Glen Melville - Special Agent
David Morris - Superintendent
Roger Rudolph – Assistant Superintendent

Curt Sauer – Chief Ranger
Timothy Simonds - Chief Ranger

Editors:

Butch Farabee

Words alone are not enough to thank Butch for his hard work and dedication helping me write this second edition. His comments and edits were spot on. This new book is a great improvement over the previous edition because of Butch. Thank you, thank you, thank you…

Marcy Innes

Marcy teaches Art and English at the 7th and 8th grade level at a small school in Vermont. She kept me on track and encouraged me in so many ways. Her edits and comments were exceptional. I don't know how she tolerated me when I disagreed with her on a fact or a sentence. It must be the teacher built inside her. She is a remarkable woman and I love her very much.

SRC = Submerged Resource Center

NPS = National Park Service

NP = National Park

INTRODUCTION

The story you are about to read is true. The names have not been changed nor have the dates or places. The characters are all real people. The places are real, and the facts are true to the best of my knowledge. Between May 2001 and December 2004, one of the goals of the Olympic National Park Dive Team was to solve the mystery of "The Missing Ones", an missing persons case from 1929, by combining archaeology, technical diving, criminal investigation and incident management. It was a challenge to combine skills and the personalities of the team. Every diver I have ever met has an ego including me. That is the nature of divers.

What I attempted to do in this investigation was perform tasks in a logical sequence and not get too far ahead of one part of the investigation over another, potentially missing clues. In cases like this, one clue can lead to other clues that branch into many directions. It is also important not to miss clues, especially the big ones. When we found a clue, we spent a fair amount of time evaluating it, looking at the clue from many angles to figure out how it fits into the mystery.

Like land search and rescue, underwater search and rescue can be a big challenge, even to the most skilled diver. In land search and rescue, searchers are trained to look in places that may be hiding clues such as decision points on trails, track traps, campsites, and stream crossings. In this underwater case, we had to figure out where the clues would be. Once we found the approximate location of the 1929 accident, we began to collect clues faster than we could evaluate them. For a time, the problem wasn't a lack of clues, but too many. It then became a matter of figuring out which clues were relevant and which were not.

Why did we tackle this case after so many years had passed? The clues and evidence should have disappeared long ago. But they didn't. I've heard it has been said many times, "Lake Crescent does not give up her secrets easily." In part, it was the challenge and the adventure that drew us to take this case. On the surface (no pun intended), it seemed almost impossible to solve. How could we possibly find clues that were 72 years old and underwater! The more I looked into the case, studying intangible clues, reading old newspaper articles, and talking to Bob Caso, the more I became convinced that something special would happen with this case. Was it a premonition?

Most Rangers never even hear about cases like this, much less get a chance to work on one. I was fortunate to be in the right place at the right time and with people who had the right skills.

Like most incidents, not one factor was responsible for creating it, but rather a series of contributing factors that all merged at one focal point. Think about a traffic accident. The road is wet, has curves, is narrow, and you're tired, your tires are worn and the traffic is heavy. You have distractions, like your cell phone or the radio, and are not giving full time and attention to your driving. You get into a car accident. Each factor contributed to the accident. If you remove just one of the factors, perhaps the accident would not have happened.

This case was solved because the volunteers, Rangers, divers, family members, the Press and Park staff were all contributing factors that merged at a focal point. Each person contributed something special that ultimately led to a success outcome. It was truly a team effort

1

A SPECIAL VISITOR

My District Ranger Office was a room about six feet by eight feet. It had a small desk stacked with search and rescue manuals and a half a dozen law books. After twenty-two years in the National Park Service, some would think my position would end up with a mahogany desk, an administrative assistant, and a six-figure income. The reality was a worn-out set of knees from lots of hiking, a cheap veneer-topped desk with a metal green-colored government chair, beat-up desktop computer, a well-used rain parka draped over my desk chair, and a mid-50s income. I wasn't complaining however. Above this desk hung a picture of my identical twin brother and me in our hockey gear. It was easy to tell us apart. He was the skinnier guy. But outside the window of my office was the real payoff for working as a National Park Ranger; there was the forest and lakes and all that wild country. I had an incredible view of Lake Crescent from my office window. My drive around Lake Crescent each morning to work was a trip surrounded by a forest primeval. That drive alone was worth considerably more to me than a mahogany desk and six-figure income.

As of April 11, 2001, I had never heard of Blanche and Russell Warren. But a series of events was about to change all that. It was a typical April day with a sky full of clouds and low fifties temperature. April and May were the months to see rainbows at Lake Crescent, and as the weather transitions from winter to spring, one can experience most climates in one day. I saw a phone message from Dr. Paul Gleeson, the park's chief for cultural resources. I had a good working relationship with Paul, probably because I had a keen interest in history and archeology and a personal link to the State of Maine, which Paul seemed to be very fond of. The note indicated he wanted me to call a man named Bob Caso. I didn't recognize the name, so I called Paul and asked who Mr. Caso was and what he wanted to talk about. He stated that Bob Caso had an interesting story to tell me about the waters of Lake Crescent. I had a feeling the phone call to Bob Caso might be an interesting one. So he had an interesting story about Lake Crescent? In the six years I had been stationed at the Lake District, I'd heard many strange stories about underwater forests, sunken boats and barges, and missing people. Thus far, I had only seen a few bits of evidence to suggest any of these tales were true. I chalked them up to urban (or rural) legends, embellished many times over a campfire and a few select adult beverages.

I was still more than a little intrigued as I reached for the phone. I liked to hear stories, even if they were a just a bit on the wild side. I dialed the number, and the phone rang four times before the answering machine picked it up with a prompt to leave a message. As soon as I began my message, the phone suddenly sprang to life with a real voice. It was Bob Caso. Bob started talking quickly. It was obvious he was anxious to share his story. He said he was a former scuba diver and had made many dives in Lake Crescent. He wanted to meet to show me maps and a file folder of newspaper articles he had collected over the years. I would later learn that Bob was a well-known figure at park headquarters in Port Angeles. He was a retired longshoreman and veteran of the Navy. I could also tell from his accent he was originally from the Mid-Atlantic States, perhaps New Jersey or New York. We talked for about 15 minutes, with him telling me how deep the lake was and a few tales of people who had disappeared and were never recovered from the lake. He certainly had my attention, and I was anxious to hear more stories about Lake Crescent. We agreed to meet a few days later.

On April 13, 2001, Bob showed up in my office at the Storm King Ranger Station at about noon. He was in his late seventies, medium height and weight, and a slight limp in his walk. He wore glasses, an Irish driving cap and leaned forward and to the left when he walked. There was warmth and sincerity in his handshake. He used a lot of voice inflections, which came across in a kind of singsong manner that matches his rich, quick laugh and lighthearted personality. Under one arm, he carried a roll of maps. In the opposite hand, a thick file folder.

2

Bob was anxious to share his story. He had been told I was the park's Dive Officer, and as fellow divers, we were immediately on common ground. We sat down in the front room of the Storm King Ranger Station surrounded by a stone fireplace, historic furniture, and a very large Beardslee trout mounted on a plaque on the wall. The Ranger Station, one of the oldest structures in the park, was a rather fitting place to hear Bob Caso's story. Bob showed me a series of old newspaper clippings. The dates were all from the summer of 1929, mostly taken from the *Port Angeles Evening News*, the most popular newspaper for the northern Olympic Peninsula from that period.

The first few articles told of two people missing from their home near Forks, Washington. The stories stated that Blanche and Russell Warren, in their mid-thirties, had disappeared while driving from nearby Port Angeles, Washington, to their home in Quillayute Prairie. The date they reportedly disappeared was July 3, 1929. The first articles were dated from mid-July 1929, and the latest from 1984. All dealt with the Warrens and the investigation of their unsolved disappearance.

My first impression was one of surprise that I had never heard this story before. My second thought was that this case had probably been solved in 1929 and simply hadn't been reported in the newspapers. But still, much like the way my Border Collie search dog "alerts" to a human scent of interest, I found myself "alerting" to Bob's story. If this was an unsolved case, then perhaps some good, old-fashioned investigative work on my part would solve it. This incident was a part of the historical, cultural, and archaeological fabric of Olympic National Park, and it was my job as a Ranger to investigate and preserve the story. Besides, it sounded like a fun project.

Some of the newspaper articles from mid-July 1929 were found on the front page or a few pages back. But the August 1929 articles were in large, bold text on the front page. It seemed the story had captured the imagination of the local population in 1929. I asked Bob if I could copy the articles and then return them later. At first he was reluctant to release his precious file, and in hindsight, I can't blame him. I copied some of the most relevant articles and made my own folder, titling it the "Warren Case." As Bob was leaving, I promised I would read the material and contact him very soon.

That night while I was in bed, I dug out the file and began reading the articles. The articles told of two boys, Charles, age twelve, and Frank, age fourteen, who were left behind after the accident. I tried to put myself in their shoes. What were their lives like after they learned their parents would likely never return home? Were the two boys still alive? Did they have children? Would there still be people around who could remember the incident of 1929?

I got out of bed to search the pages of the North Olympic Peninsula phonebook for Frank or Charles Warren, the two sons. There they were! Could it possibly be the two boys were living right here in Port Angeles? A few days later, I called both of them and discovered that these two people had no relationship to the Warrens who disappeared many years ago. Yet it was ironic they were listed in the North Olympic phone book. It was a strange beginning. Thus began the journey that would change the lives of many people, including myself.

2

IN THE BEGINNING

Lake Crescent is in the northwest corner of Washington State on the Olympic Peninsula, within Olympic National Park. It is known for its deep aqua-colored clear waters and large Beardslee trout. The south shore of the lake is about 13 miles long. The widest section is about a mile wide and the deepest section is 624 feet deep. The name is thought to derive from its unusual crescent shape; however, others have a different story about the origin of the name.

About 20,000 years ago, the Olympic Peninsula was covered with a sheet of ice perhaps several thousand feet thick in places. Some peaks and mountains in the Olympics were actually above the ice and snow. Ocean levels were 150 to 300 feet lower than they are today, leaving large coastal lands open for people to exploit and utilize.

Lake Crescent has experienced nine separate large glacial periods over the last nine hundred thousand years. The last one ended about 11,500 years ago, commonly called the Pleistocene era. Climactic change over the past 900,000 thousand years has not always been a slow and steady process. Some climate changes have occurred in just a few hundred years and in some cases just a few decades or even years. Evidence of these global weather patterns have been found in Arctic, Antarctic, and Greenland ice cores. These climactic swings include long and short-term cold and warm periods. A strongly supported theory is that volcanoes discharged considerable amounts of ash into the atmosphere, thus creating short-term global climactic events. The release of enormous amounts of methane gas from under glacial ice or permafrost may also have contributed to short- and long-term climatic events. Various events involving the changing of ocean currents, the earth's axis, greenhouse gases, changes in the size of the Antarctic, Arctic, and polar snow and ice and rising and falling ocean levels, have all been cited as contributing to these significant climactic events.

Significant evidence suggests that North America's first occupants came from northeast Asia by foot and watercraft and ventured all the way to the southern tip of South America. This ancient journey occurred sometime between eighteen and 20,000 thousand years ago, perhaps even earlier. They were the first humans to see and discover this land. These first North American inhabitants could have made this 12,000 mile journey to the tip of South America in nine or ten generations. Imagine arriving in a land abundant with wildlife that had never seen humans before. The hunting and fishing must have been highly successful because these original settlers prospered, and became the ancestors of today's Native Americans.

The early human occupants of this new and wild land would have had to quickly change survival tactics, lifestyles and habits. They would have needed to move around the Olympic Peninsula to avoid frequent flooding and to recover from the occasional tsunami and earthquake. They were apparently highly successful and resilient in adjusting to their new home.

Archaeologists are not sure when the Olympic Peninsula was first populated. There is evidence that people had been traveling by large ocean-going canoes from Vancouver Island across the Strait of Juan de Fuca to the Olympic Peninsula coast for many centuries, long before native people were contacted by Europeans in large sailing vessels. Trading between the islands was common and well established. Hunting whales on the open ocean in these large canoes was a common practice.

People have been living on the Olympic Peninsula for 150 centuries or more. Ethnographic data reported a Klallam village, which was occupied into the later 1890s on the east end of Lake Crescent. Ethnographers in the 1930s gave this village the name East Lake Crescent. The name used by the Klallam people for Lake Crescent was Tsawlmawt, which sounds similar to crescent when pronounced in the Klallam vocalization. Perhaps this was the origin of the name for Lake

Crescent. The native word KLce'nt ce'yell, also having a similar pronunciation to Crescent when pronounced in the native style, was the general term used by the Klallam tribe for any lake. It is possible that the European settlers heard the name in reference to the lake and then spelled it in the English language as it was pronounced by the natives. Many words in Olympic Peninsula Indian language have a hard K sound: Quinault, Kalaloch, Queets, Clallam, and Makah, to name a few.

Others believe the name Lake Crescent was derived from nearby Crescent Bay (to the north on the shores of the Straits of Juan de Fuca), so named by Captain Henry Kellett in 1846. In 1849, two Canadian trappers named John Sutherland and John Everett, who were reportedly the first Europeans to visit the two nearby lakes, were credited with renaming them. They reportedly hiked in from Crescent Bay and found two neighboring lakes, naming them after themselves. John Everett was supposedly the larger of the two men and named the larger of the two lakes after himself. It is possible that John Everett acknowledged the local Indian name, or perhaps his naming of the lake was just forgotten. About twenty years later, Lake Everett appears as Lake Crescent on maps and reference material. The name Lake Sutherland stuck and remains to this day.

Lake Crescent was a place for spiritual discovery and vision for the native Klallam people. One account describes a man who held a large boulder in his arms and jumped into a deep hole in the lake, sinking to the bottom. Another account (perhaps false) stated that the Klallam people never ventured into the Olympic Mountains and never used Lake Crescent because the area contained evil spirits. The lake was said to swallow people and never give them back. As noted in a 1996 Lower Elwha Klallam calendar, tribal children were told to *"have great respect for Lake Crescent, for it was where many unexplainable things happened."*

The Klallam people tell a story about their ancestors who lived near Lake Crescent. According to their legend, the Klallam and Quillayute tribes were fighting along a small river at Lake Crescent (this could have been the ancient inlet of Lake Sutherland from Lake Crescent at the far western end of Lake Sutherland). After three days of fighting, the ruler of Mount Storm King became furious at the warriors fighting below him and threw down a piece of the mountain, burying and killing many warriors and separating the fighting tribes.

Physical evidence of a massive landslide on the far southeast end of Lake Crescent suggests that the legend may be true. There is evidence of two massive landslides on the southeastern end of Lake Crescent, where the lake meets the descending ridgeline of Mt. Storm King. However, the largest slide and perhaps the one that had the greatest impact on Lake Crescent came from the north.

Lake Crescent – June 2002 – Courtesy of Olympic National Park Dive Team.

The ancient small, river inlet into Lake Sutherland mentioned in the story was buried by the landslide, damming Lake Crescent. Govin's Hill, on the east end of Lake Crescent, which U.S. Highway 101 traverses, is part of that ancient landslide. Today, Lake Crescent is 83 feet higher than Lake Sutherland in elevation because of the natural dam at Govin's Hill. The outlet of Lake Crescent is now the Lyre River on the northeast end of the lake. The Lyre River Canyon shows evidence of erosion from only recently in geological time and is much younger than other nearby rivers and canyons that show much older evidence of erosion.

Ancient submerged trees found in Lake Crescent in 2003 and 2004 by our dive team were cored and dated using tree rings, providing evidence that the landslides occurred 5,990 years ago. These large landslides from Mt. Storm King could have been triggered by earthquakes and is evidence of ancient mega earthquakes as powerful as 9.0 or greater on the Richter Scale.

European explorers who came to western Washington and Oregon in the mid-1840s did not begin to settle with native people until about 1850. Small towns began to spring up around the coast of the Olympic Peninsula. Port Townsend was the largest city in the Washington Territory until 1890, when Seattle surpassed it in population. This was due in part to the railroad coming to Seattle instead of Port Townsend. Around 1890, people of European origin began arriving by boat on the Washington coast in small numbers and ventured into such places as Lake Ozette, the Hoh, Lake Quinault and Lake Crescent. Some hiked into these areas, and others hired local natives to take them by canoe.

The deep interior of the Olympic Mountains was largely unknown to the new settlers. Several explorations of the interior, one was sponsored by the Seattle Press newspaper company and written about in Seattle newspapers, opened the minds of many settlers to the Olympic Peninsula. However, native people knew the interior well and had been crossing the Olympic Mountains for thousands of years. Many areas of the Olympic interior were used as hunting grounds following ancient travel routes.

Many of today's trails and roads on the Olympic Peninsula began as games and hunting trails. There were literally hundreds, if not thousands, of miles of trails on the Olympic Peninsula, and not a single tree was ever cut to clear a trail. When obstacles were encountered, ancient travelers simply found a route around them. When horses and wagons arrived in the late 1880s, these trails were improved. When automobiles finally arrived about 1905, the trails were further improved and eventually roads were constructed that wagons and the new cars could travel on.

In 1896, President Cleveland created the Olympic Forest Reserve in an effort to manage the lands for timber production and development. Lake Crescent was included in this Reserve. Prior to this, people could make claims on open and unclaimed land in 160-acre parcels as authorized under Federal law passed during the Lincoln administration. Many did not even bother to register claims. They just simply found a place to build a cabin and settled in. If someone else happened to own the land, a land dispute would seldom be initiated. Land was cheap and easy to come by. These illegal settlers were referred to as squatters.

Chris Morgenroth, a native of Germany, arrived in western Washington in the spring of 1890. He staked a claim to land along the Bogachiel River with the intent of farming. He quickly realized that his property was not suitable for farming without a monumental effort to clear all the rocks, trees, and stumps. He stated, *"We wanted farm land... We were going to pioneer and develop the west, but there were no markets, no roads, no trails, and we did not get any for at least another thirty years."* He found work with the newly created Forest Reserve. In the river valleys of the Bogachiel and Hoh, he helped build new trails and improved existing ones. This skill later became an asset to him when hired as the first Ranger for Mt. Olympus National Monument.

Morgenroth built a cabin on the east side of Barnes Point at Lake Crescent for the Forest Reserve in 1909, according to National Park records. His daughter Katherine disputed that date and stated that with the help of Paul Laufeld, a seasonal Ranger, he built the cabin in 1903 or 1904. The Morgenroth cabin was the first Ranger station on the Peninsula. It was used to house the Morgenroth family, seasonal Rangers, and fire guards. The cabin fell into disrepair and, in 1952, was considered in "fair to poor" condition by the National Park Service. It later became the Storm King Ranger Station in the 1980s after it was restored. The cabin is the oldest structure in Olympic National Park and would later become my office.

Chris Morgenroth later built a series of Ranger Stations, three-sided shelters, over 600 miles of hiking trails, and many bridges across the wild rivers of the interior. These stations were in central locations that served as supply bases and fire lookouts and were connected with copper radiophone lines strung through the trees.

Other important pioneers included Harry, Edward, and George Brooks who arrived on the Peninsula in 1910 from their native England by way of Canada. Edward homesteaded forty acres of land on the northeast end of Lake Crescent at Piedmont. In 1915, Edward Brooks, a Forest Ranger under Chris Morgenroth, lived with his family in the cabin built by Morgenroth. Edward Brooks later became the proprietor of the La Poel Resort on Lake Crescent. Harry left for Seattle, later returning with a wife. George Brooks lived near Ovington on the northwest end of Lake Crescent, and worked as a deckhand on the Lake Crescent ferry, *The Marjory*.

In 1909, Mt. Olympus National Monument was created by powers granted to the president under the Antiquities Act of 1906. Two days before Theodore Roosevelt left office, he signed a Presidential Proclamation creating Mt. Olympus National Monument. The document, written by one of Roosevelt's closest advisors, Gifford Pinchot, was vague and offered little protection to the elk herds it was intended to protect. Lake Crescent was included in the new National Monument.

From about 1905 to 1922, traveling from Port Angeles to Forks, a distance of about sixty miles was difficult. One could travel by boat over the open Pacific Ocean into the Strait of Juan de Fuca, by horse and buggy, using the ferry service on Lake Crescent, or by taking a very long hike. Ferry service was available on Lake Crescent from the East Beach Resort at the far eastern end of the lake to the Fairholm Resort on the far western end of the lake. The ferryboat would make several stops along the way: Singer Tavern, Rose Mary Inn, Ovington Resort, Keith Wallace Resort and perhaps at a few private cabins.

Taken in about 1925, this is Sledgehammer Point on the shores of Lake Crescent. Note the wheel of a car. Courtesy of the Olympic National Park.

The best known boats were the Storm King and the Marjory, and later, the Betty Earls. These ferries delivered mail and provided transport for wagons and tourists who wished to visit the Sol Duc Hot Springs and resorts previously mentioned. The Hot Springs were a popular attraction in the early days, but travel was a difficult horse ride, wagon ride, or hike into the nearby Sol Duc Valley. A trail and road were eventually constructed a few miles west of the end of Lake Crescent, creating a link between the Fairholm Resort ferry dock and the Sol Duc Resort.

In 1922, when the Olympic Highway was finally opened for vehicle traffic, ferry service on Lake Crescent came to an end. Vehicles could now drive from Port Angeles to the town of Forks and back in one day. Log trucks quickly saw the opportunity to haul logs on the new road. The road was somewhat unforgiving and a challenge to even the best of vehicles and drivers. The first vehicles had to negotiate a single-lane road with turnouts. Vehicle traffic was relatively low at first as most people still did not own cars. Cars were expensive for the day and subject to numerous breakdowns. Tires were cut, bruised, and battered by the rough roads. Flat tires were very common. Many cars carried two spare tires in addition to a hand-crank jack, tire-patch kit, air pump, and assorted wrenches and screwdrivers.

Improvements to the highway around Lake Crescent over the years have increased driver safety. It had been widened to accommodate faster speeds and wider trucks and cars. Many of the roadside turnouts seen today were once part of the original road. Many of the curves have guardrail protection, preventing vehicles from leaving the roadway and plunging into the lake. The road, in many places, has been elevated to a level that is now well above the Lake. Even with all these improvements, motor vehicle accidents, sometimes serious, still occur, suggesting that no road can be built that will prevent all accidents.

From 1896 to 1912, Paul Barnes owned 135 acres of land near the Ranger Station at Barnes Point. This property included the creek and delta "formed by an extinct glacier."

Here he built the Marymere Hotel and gave his surname to the creek, point, and "glacier" (it is interesting to note that there were still the remnants of an ancient glacier in the Barnes Creek drainage at the turn of the 20th century). Barnes sold land to Thomas Aldwell, a developer, who built a house and subdivided the lots. In November of 1927, Aldwell sold two lots to Harry Brooks and his wife, Augusta Erickson Brooks. The lots were south of the recently built Olympic Highway.

The Brooks family built an inn, restaurant, and store on the property and lived in the inn. They opened for business in the summer of 1929 and named the establishment the *Storm King Inn*. Harry's sister, Daisy Brooks Firkins, and her husband, Arthur, were partners in the endeavor, but the partnership lasted only 2 years. Augusta Brooks brought considerable cooking, baking and caretaker skills to the new business. News quickly spread that their restaurant had the best food on the Lake. Harry Brooks later added four small cabins and rented them to tourists. Years later the National Park Service bought the Inn and used it, renaming it the *Storm King Ranger Station*. The Inn was located across the road from the present Storm King Ranger Station (the 1986 restored Morgenroth cabin). Harry and his brother Ed become important players in helping to solve the several mysteries around Lake Crescent, including *The Missing Ones*, the story of the disappearance of Blanche and Russell Warren, as we shall see in the chapters ahead.

Above is the new Storm King Inn on the south side of the Olympic Highway about 1930. Olympic National Park would not be created for another 8 years. At the time of this picture, much of the surrounding forest was within Olympic National Monument administered by the U.S. Forest Service and part of Olympic National Forest. Note the large trees in the background. Courtesy of Olympic National Park.

3

MYSTERIOUS LAKE CRESCENT

Over the past one hundred years, there have been many incidents on the waters of Lake Crescent, probably more then we know. Some of the victims were presumed to have drowned, but do we really know what happened to them? In several cases, searchers were lucky enough to recover the victim(s), and in one case, a body was miraculously recovered several years later.

Steep underwater slopes, vertical cliffs and water depths of several hundred feet near the shore and the edge of the roadway increase the risk of traumatic accidentals. These underwater geological features also increase the challenge for search teams. The deepest point of Lake Crescent is 624 feet on the west end of the Lake, directly north of Wallace Point in the middle of the Lake. These depths are simply too deep recreational scuba divers. Only highly specialized technical divers can reach these depths.

Until recently, underwater search and rescue technologies were primitive. Today underwater investigators have tools such as deep diving submersible submarines, deep-water technical divers, side-scan sonar, LIDAR (an aerial digital laser mapping system), magnetometers, and remote-operated vehicles (ROVs). However, even with these technologies investigators are still looking for a needle in a haystack and only with a moderate probability of success. The waters of the world, including Lake Crescent, remain as mysterious as ever.

A common weather condition on lakes such as Lake Crescent is a very-predictable afternoon wind. Depending on air temperature and local topography, warm summer air rises off the surrounding mountains, land and water. Cooler air will come in from the west and the east ends of the Lake to replace the rising warm air, creating a lake-surface wind. This surface wind can turn the Lake from as smooth as glass at 9:00 a.m. to a 3 foot tight chop by noon. Boaters, motorized and non-motorized, can find navigation a considerable challenge. Row boats and canoes experiencing these wind conditions may have to seek shore or a safe harbor. Sailboat owners search for these winds and relish them with considerable enjoyment. These winds were likely a contributing factor in a number of the following cases.

This map of Lake Crescent is from the Olympic National Park brochure. Courtesy of Olympic National Park.

Hallie Latham Illingsworth – The Lady Of The Lake

On July 6, 1940, two fishermen found a body floating on the surface of Lake Crescent. It turned out to be the body of Hallie Latham Illingsworth, missing since a few days before Christmas in 1937. She had been wrapped in blankets; her arms and legs tied with heavy rope. The story captivated local citizens evidence suggested that she had been beaten and strangled. Her body apparently floated to the surface of Lake Crescent when the ropes that were used to secure heavy weights to her body rotted away or the knots came loose. The cold waters and the unique chemistry and temperature of the lake helped preserve her remains. Her body had "*saponified*," or as some would say, "*turned to soap.*" She would later be named *The Lady of the Lake*.

Hallie and her second husband, Monty Illingsworth, were known to be heavy drinkers and reportedly had frequent and violent fights. After the disappearance of his wife, Monty then vanished and was discovered living in southern California with the daughter of a successful Port Angeles auto dealer. He was later arrested by Los Angeles County Sheriffs, extradited to Clallam County, charged with the murder of his wife, and convicted. Harry Brooks was a key witness at the trial, testifying that he gave Monty a cut length of heavy rope, a piece of which Brooks still had, and which was later identified as the rope used to tie up Hallie. Harry Books would later play a critical role in the Warren case.

Arthur Stetson

Shortly before 1:00 p.m. on June 17, 1945, Arthur Stetson, age twenty-seven, departed from East Beach on the east end of Lake Crescent in his outboard-driven pleasure boat. He was reportedly en route to the summer cabin of Mr. and Mrs. Donald H. Lutz (Arthur's brother-in-law). Their cabin was about four miles away in Barnes Cove. Earlier that day, Mr. Lutz had driven Stetson, Stetson's wife, Florence (Lutz), a daughter, and two sons (one of which was named Lawrence) to East Beach where the boat was moored. Lutz dropped off Stetson and then drove himself and the rest of the Stetson family to Barnes Cove. The plan was for Stetson to motor the boat back to Barnes Cove and meet the family back at their cabin.

A short time later, Stetson's boat was found east of Rocky Point (Sledgehammer Point), drifting, with no one aboard and with the motor turned off. Despite wide media coverage, no witnesses of the incident came forward. The newspaper stories presumed that he had drowned in the Lake. Clallam County Deputy Sheriff Karl Kirk, along with many volunteers, started a search immediately, but what happened to Arthur Stetson remains a mystery.

Grant (Bud) Girt and Les Getchell

On June 24, 1949, two fishermen presumably drowned in Lake Crescent near La Poel picnic area. Their names were Leslie F. Getchell, age forty-five, of Port Angeles (a big strapping guy and "good outdoors man," according to Bob Caso) and Wilbert "Grant" or "Bud" Girt, age thirty-three, also of Port Angeles. The two men left Port Angeles about 4:30 p.m. en route to Lake Crescent to go fishing. They launched their boat at the Keith Wallace cottage where later the brother-in-law of Girt found and identified the trailer and vehicle. It was believed they drowned in the lake when they tried to get back to shore, probably due to the late afternoon or evening winds.

A U.S. Coast Guard helicopter (a new program for the Coast Guard in those days) searched the waters of Lake Crescent, assisted by Olympic National Park Rangers. Chief Ranger Otto Brown was the lead investigator for the Park. Their fishing boat was found adrift near shore at La Poel, east of where they had launched. Gear and motor were aboard, but they were not. An extensive search by Rangers revealed no clues, and the search was called off after several days. Divers were reportedly never deployed. District Ranger W.K. Merrill and Seasonal Ranger Louis Messmer assisted with the search effort. A passing truck driver who was a close friend of the two saw them fishing near Wallace Point at 5:15 p.m. Their bodies were never recovered, and what happened to the two fishermen remains a mystery to this day.

Tommy Lyons

On Sunday, August 9, 1983, Tommy Wayne Lyons, age 33, his wife, Robin, age 26 and stepson, Darrell, age 6, arrived at Wallace Point at Lake Crescent at about two in the afternoon. They came to the Lake to enjoy an afternoon of sun and swimming. Tommy was employed as a truck driver for the Hoh River Timber Company in Beaver, a small town a few miles west of Lake Crescent. Shortly before coming to the lake, they bought a few hamburgers and had a lunch picnic in Lincoln Park in the city of Port Angeles. While at La Poel, a popular destination on the shores of the Lake, they lugged a cooler and food down to the thin strip of the beach. This was rather typical of a mid-summer day at the Lake, sunny with air temperatures in the mid 70's and a 5 to 10 miles-per-hour wind out of the north creating a light surface chop. The water temperature was about sixty degrees at the surface, but much colder just a few feet below the surface.

Young Darrell was playing on the beach with a large truck inner tube and rolled it into the lake. The wind caught the tube and pushed it in a northwest direction off shore at about a 45 degree angle. Tommy followed the inner tube for a short distance from shore and decided to change into his Levi shorts in hopes of swimming out to the inner tube to retrieve it. He reportedly dipped himself into the water several times to get used to the cold water and then plunged into the lake, swimming a short distance underwater. Robin stated that Tommy was a strong swimmer and had been swimming in the Lake many times before. She stated as Tommy swam out to the inner tube, he tried to grab it but missed it a couple of times. She reportedly followed his progress by walking along the shoreline. She stated that after he missed the inner tube, she saw him roll over on his back at which time she yelled at him asking if he was OK. She stated that he did not respond. Robin said that she ran up to the road to wave down passing tourists for assistance. When a vehicle finally stopped, she turned around to spot where her husband had been but could no longer see him. The vehicle that stopped contained two local citizens named David Feeley and Larry Thomas. Feeley later told Park Rangers that he saw the inner tube floating on the water as they approached Wallace Point but never saw a person near it. Feeley later told Rangers that Robin told him that her husband had disappeared 35 to 50 yards from shore.

News of the accident was transmitted by CB radio and overheard by the proprietor of the Fairholm Store, Betty Ketchum. Betty called the Park Rangers stationed at the Lake. Rangers Michael Butler and Larry Lang arrived at the scene at 2:19 p.m. and directed Rangers Art Sandison and John Ward to respond with scuba-diving gear in the park patrol boat. The divers arrived on scene at 2:30 p.m. Ranger Butler told the divers that the incident would be treated like a cold-water-drowning case. If the divers were able to retrieve Lyons, resuscitation efforts would be made. At 2:24 p.m. Ranger Butler summoned an ambulance thinking that Tommy Lyons would be found quickly.

The divers descended into the depths of the lake about 50 yards east of the point Tommy was reportedly last seen and searched in a westerly direction at depths of 120, 100, and 80 feet. A second dive followed this one, searching shallower water. Additional dive gear and divers were brought to the scene. Ranger divers Ward, Lang, Butler and Sandison continued to search underwater in shifts until 8:15 p.m. without finding Lyons. Divers continued the search the next day until 3:00 p.m., searching the primary search area east and west of the point last seen. Lyons was still missing and presumed drowned. On the very first dive, Rangers Sandison and Ward did find an important clue. They found what appeared to be impressions in the soft, shallow mud bottom at a depth of about 110 feet. The impressions appeared to be fresh and descended into deeper water beyond the maximum depth (130 feet) of the divers' training. Ranger Lang described the impressions as appearing to be footprints.

On Tuesday, August 11, four deep-water technical divers from Puget Sound Commercial Divers and a local Port Angeles dive shop dove to two hundred feet in depth, following the tracks. The tracks continued down beyond two hundred feet in depth. The divers concluded that the only plausible explanation for the tracks were that the victim must have hit the bottom feet first and left tracks as he continued to sink into the depths of the lake on the steep slope. Diver John Sweatt reported that the water temperature below one hundred feet was a cool thirty-eight degrees.

On Monday, August 17, Olympic National Park Law Enforcement Specialist Woody Jones received information from the Port Angeles Police Department that property belonging to Tommy Lyons had been turned in. The property included two drivers' licenses, one each from Washington and Alaska, a Teamster's ID card, and other Teamster papers and business cards from Lyon's Security. The property was reportedly found in a water-meter box at 1808 West Fifth Street, a few houses east of Tommy Lyon's residence at 1834 West Fifth Street. According to Robin's statement, she believed that Tommy's wallet containing forty dollars was in his Levi cutoffs, since she could not find it in the car at the scene or at their residence. She further stated that her husband had no known medical conditions that would have contributed to his death. No clues or witnesses were discovered that would explain how Tommy's wallet ended up in the water-meter box. The case was suspended due to a lack of new clues. Tommy Lyons is presumed to be in Lake Crescent at a depth beyond what divers could safely reach in 1983.

The following cases occurred on the west end of Lake Crescent. That end of the lake would later be in the area of interest of the Olympic National Park Dive Team as the search for the Warrens progressed.

THE MISSING ONES

Russell W. Heuhsliem

On Friday, November 5, 1954, at about 7:00 p.m., a pickup truck driven by Russell W. Heuhsliem, age 37, spun out of control while traveling east near Meldrim Point carrying Russell to his death. Divers John Sweatt and Richard Owens retrieved the truck with Russell's body still in it the next morning from fifteen feet of water. Witnesses reported they could see headlights from the truck two hours after the accident. Olympic National Park Chief Ranger John F. Alton was in charge of the recovery operation assisted by local Rangers, the county sheriffs, and state patrol officers.

Ernest Dahlgran

On Friday, August 25, 1956, at 3:26 p.m., an ambulance owned by Peninsula Ambulance Service traveling east toward Port Angeles never made it to the hospital. The ambulance carrying Ernest Dahlgran, age 56, a logger with a suspected fractured leg sustained in a logging show, plunged into Lake Crescent at Meldrim Point. The ambulance attendants caring for the injured Dahlgran were identified as Charles Ecklund, age 18, James Harlow, and Stan Bigelow, all from Port Angeles. The driver was Joseph Thomas. Ecklund stated that the ambulance was traveling at a normal speed, when he heard the brakes begin to squeal. The vehicle was tossed around and then began to fill with water. Ecklund said that he couldn't swim but did manage to break out a window and crawl out of the ambulance. He said he tried to help the injured logger in the back of the ambulance, but because he could not swim, he was not able to help him. He came to the surface a short distance from shore and was pulled from the Lake by two loggers who witnessed the accident. The two unidentified loggers again entered the water and pulled to shore an unconscious man they had seen floating on the surface. The unconscious man was the driver, Joseph Thomas, age 52. Ecklund, Harlow, and Bigelow performed artificial respiration on Thomas. All four were taken to the Olympic Memorial Hospital for treatment. Ecklund, Harlow, and Bigelow were released from the hospital that evening. Incredibly, Joseph Thomas survived the accident and was later released from the hospital.

Scuba divers from Port Angeles, John Sweatt, Lewis Sample, and William Wilson, recovered Dahlgran's body from 90 feet of water, found just outside the ambulance. The ambulance was found in 150 feet of water and 200 feet from shore. An investigation revealed skid marks that showed that the ambulance failed to negotiate the curve, struck a tree on the lakeside of the road, then hit a second tree before rolling into the water. Divers reported underwater debris scattered on the slope where the ambulance rolled into the lake and indicated that the ambulance rolled end over end into the depths of the lake. Divers attached a rope to the ambulance and removed it from the lake.

William Contesti

On Friday, October 26, 1956, at about 7:30 p.m., a pickup truck driven by William Contesti failed to make the curve at Meldrim Point and plunged into the lake, a short distance from shore. Contesti and his passenger, Kenneth Henderson, quickly escaped the confines of the truck and survived.

Dale, Dee Dee, Beverly and Gary

On the night of January 24, 1960, driver Dale Steele, age 22, Diane "Dee Dee" Cowles, age 22, Gary Lind, age 22, and Beverly Sherman, age 20, were in a 1950 Dodge two-door sedan headed east toward Port Angeles. As they rounded a curve, one and a half miles east of Fairholm, the car reportedly slid on a patch of ice, failed to make a curve a few hundred feet east of Meldrim Point, and slid into the dark cold waters of Lake Crescent. Dale and Gary managed first to escape the sinking car. Beverly, who sustained cuts to her face after having struck the windshield, was next to surface. Beverley and Gary were able to swim and find the shore in nearly complete darkness. But Dee Dee had not surfaced yet. In desperation, Dale dove into the inky-black water, trying to reach the sinking car, hoping to rescue her. He made three dives without reaching an unknown depth to where the car was headed. When he surfaced after the third dive, he saw Dee Dee pop to the surface a short distance away and swim to shore. Gathering together after their frightening ordeal, all four walked a short distance on the road and were picked up by the driver of a passing log truck. Beverly received stitches to her face, and all survived their harrowing, near-fatal accident. Their car disappeared into the depths of Lake Crescent. Local diver, John Sweatt, was again summoned to the scene and dove to a depth of 150 feet and reported the car fell off a steep cliff at about 100 feet and into an unknown depth. He saw a car mirror at about 150 feet. Beverly reported the car was full of possessions for her upcoming twenty-first birthday and had travel luggage in the trunk related to a recent trip to New York.

On July 4, 2003, Beverly Sherman came to Lake Crescent at my invitation. I took her back to the accident scene of 43 years ago. I asked her to walk and drive the road with me in an effort to relive the near tragedy. She was able to tell me exactly where the car had left the roadway. She told me the roadway had once been where the small roadside turnout was east of Meldrim Point.

It just so happened that two friends of mine, Dale and Ed Jacobs, were at the Lake that weekend and were experimenting with their new ROV (remote operated underwater vehicle). I called them and asked them if they were willing to experiment with their new ROV searching the area identified by Beverly. They found the 1950 Dodge in two hundred feet of water in about 30 minutes using the camera of the ROV. Beverly Sherman was given the once-in-a-lifetime opportunity to revisit the car. The Jacobs took Beverley Sherman aboard their boat and provided her with video goggles, while the ROV toured the car, thus allowing her to go back to the car that nearly took her life, so many years ago.

A few days later, technical divers, Art Sandison Bill Walker and I searched the lake bottom to a depth of 210 feet. We found the car in 197 feet of water and retrieved a hubcap. I returned to the owner of the car, Dale Steele, who was waiting on shore at the time. Several months later, a volunteer dive team led by Bill Walker, with special assistance from Dale and Ed Jacobs (who were able to open the trunk assisted by the ROV) recovered and returned all of the possessions that were in the car including clothes, books, and jewelry. Dale and Dee Dee Steele (now married) and Beverley Sherman were at the scene when divers surfaced with their possessions. *Inside Edition*, The New York news magazine television show, came to Lake Crescent on that weekend and documented the story in a program called *"What Lies Beneath."*

Roberta Phinney

On Saturday, August 16, 1975, Roberta Phinney, age 32, her son Thomas, age 4, and her daughter Sally, age 3, were traveling along the shores of Lake Crescent on Highway 101. The roadway was wet from recent rains in a normally dry summer. Investigating Ranger, Bill Ferraro, reported that Roberta missed the East Beach Road near the east end of the lake that would have taken her toward Agate-Crescent Beach along the Straits of Juan De Fuca where she was to have met her husband and son Christopher. She realized her mistake when she drove to the far west end of the lake and began to double back toward the East Beach road. The vehicle, reportedly traveling too fast for the conditions, missed a sharp curve one mile east of Fairholm and plunged into the lake. A resident across the lake saw the car plunge into the lake and called the sheriff's office who called the Rangers. The park dive team recovered all three victims, but resuscitation efforts failed.

Ranger Thomas

In the early morning hours of December 29, 1983, a family of five in a small sedan was traveling east on Highway 101 around Lake Crescent and lost control on a reportedly slick roadway. The investigation revealed the car did a 180 degree spin and slid into thirty feet of ice-cold water. The mother, father, and four-year-old daughter managed to escape the car and swim to shore. However a five-year-old daughter and twenty-month-old son were still trapped inside the vehicle. Off-duty Lake Crescent Ranger Richard Thomas received a phone call at his nearby residence (Barnes Point), reporting the accident. He immediately donned his wet suit, grabbed his already packed dive gear, and amazingly arrived at the scene ten minutes later. He was told of the two trapped children and knew that he had to act quickly if there was any chance to save the children in these cold water conditions.

Extremely cold water increases the chance of survival due to a phenomenon known as the *Mammalian Effect*. The body, when immersed very quickly in extremely cold water shuts down the surface and extremity circulation. It then shunts warm blood to the core of the body and the brain in an attempt to preserve core body temperature. Respirations and heartbeat slow down to a point that they are almost impossible to detect without special equipment. People have been raised from very cold-water-drowning situations and have been successfully rewarmed and revived. The longest known cold-water-drowning survivor had been underwater for over one hour!

Ranger Thomas splashed into the icy waters of the lake and found the car. He retrieved one child from inside the car and brought this child to shore. He quickly turned around and made a second solo dive, located the second child thirty feet away from the car in forty feet of water and brought this child to the shore. In doing so, he broke one of the cardinal rules of diving (in 1985), to never scuba dive alone. Was the risk worth the potential outcome? The answer was clearly yes. The water temperature was a dangerous 43 degrees. Nearly exhausted from the two cold water dives, he directed the resuscitation efforts of the two children while the ambulance rushed to the accident scene. Both children were transported to the hospital in Port Angeles as the life-saving efforts continued. Incredibly, both children were revived at the hospital but later died from injuries sustained in the car accident.

For his heroic deed, Ranger Richard Thomas was given the Department of Interior Valor Award, the highest recognition an employee of the Department of Interior and the National Park Service can receive. Richard W. Thomas was tragically killed in an airplane accident on June 22, 1984, while leading a search-and-rescue training mission for the Civil Air Patrol.

We really do not know how many victims of crime or accident may be in Lake Crescent. If the Lake was drained, there would likely be a few surprises!

4

THE WARREN FAMILY

The history of the Warren family dates back to 1797, when Levi Warren, the grandfather of Russell Warren, was born. He married Sally Sarah Dean, who was born in Canada and together they moved from New York to Jackson County, Wisconsin, in 1856. On their pioneering voyage west, they were accompanied by their children, of whom the youngest was Frank (the father of Russell Warren). Frank was born in Chautauqua County, New York, on June 21, 1846. Frank had thirteen other siblings, but it is not known how many children traveled to Wisconsin in 1856. The 1860 census stated Frank and his siblings Edwin and Mary were all living on a farm with their parents. In about 1864, Edwin and his father, Levi, were working the farm near Black River Falls and were attacked by a roving band of Sioux Indians. Levi received a serious injury in the attack and reportedly died from that injury a few years later on December 5, 1866.

On March 30, 1864, at the age of 17, Frank Warren enlisted in the Union Army and served in Company C of the Thirty-seventh Regiment Infantry, as a drummer boy. He was involved in the Battle of the Wilderness and then in the sieges of Richmond and Petersburg, Virginia. He was wounded in a battle at Petersburg while charging with his company. A shell fragment struck him in the face, injuring his left eye and jaw. The eye became infected and eventually he had to have it removed. After that, he wore a black eye patch. Frank served until the end of the war. It was said he wore a beard for the rest of his life in order to hide a large and deep scar on his jaw.

Frank Warren 1846-
1918. Courtesy of
the Warren family.

After the Civil War, Frank returned to Wisconsin to farm where he
met and married Harriet Miles in 1867. Nineteen years later, Harriet
passed away. They had four children, two of whom lived long lives.

In 1889, at the age of 46, Frank Warren remarried to 32 year-old
Eva-May Bishop. They produced 6 more children, 5 of whom survived
to adulthood. They were Stafford, Helen, Genevieve, Robert, Russell,
and Harriet.

Eva-May Bishop, was born in Buffalo County, Wisconsin, on June
28, 1857. She was educated in California and later taught school in
Wisconsin before her marriage to Frank.

Tragedy struck the family early when Eva-May and Frank lost their first-born son, Stafford. He was born in August 1890 and died that same year. He was killed in a strange accident while traveling from Jackson County to Clark County in a horse-drawn wagon. The horses spooked for an unknown reason and threw Eva-May and her son out of the wagon. The boy died of a concussion while Eva-May received many injuries, including a broken arm.

Eva-May and Frank had five other children. Russell was born on June 11, 1891, and farmed with his father early in his life. Helen was born on February 19, 1893, and later married John Matteson on January 19, 1914, in Wisconsin. Genevieve was born on October 2, 1895. She died on January 18, 1919. Interestingly, Genevieve died just three months after her mother. Harriet Louise was born on February 19, 1898, married Merle Pitzlin, and died in 1968 in Tampa, Florida. The sixth child was Robert Warren.

The back of this photo was labeled "RCW" and is likely a picture of Russell Collins Warren, son of Frank Warren and Eva May Bishop. Courtesy of the Warren Family.

Frank died of tuberculosis at his home on German Hill in Black River Falls Wisconsin on January 6, 1918. In the Jackson County Journal, dated January 16, 1918, Frank was described as, "*a good soldier and a good citizen at all times. He was a likable and approachable man and lived on friendly terms with all. He was honest and straightforward in all his transactions and liberal and generous in his dealing with his fellow* men." The newspaper described him as being five feet and four and a quarter inches tall, with blue eyes and dark hair.

Eva-May died on September 26, 1918, a mere 9 months after her husband Frank, at the home of her daughter, Genevieve, in Irish Valley, Wisconsin. Her death certificate recorded that she died of tuberculosis and diabetes.

Russell Warren married Blanche Rhone in a double wedding ceremony on January 11, 1915. Russell's middle sister, Genevieve, married George W. June on the same day. Russell was described as an "*honest, industrious young man*" while Blanche was described as a "*worthy young lady*." Russell and Blanche quickly began their family. Their first son, Frank Russell Warren, was born in March 15, 1915. Charles Venning Warren was born on October 4, 1916. Both boys were born in Wisconsin. A third child, a daughter, died while still an infant. Russell, Blanche and the two boys moved to Rapalje, Montana, sometime in early 1918. Russell attended his mother's funeral in Wisconsin in September of 1918, traveling from Rapalje, Montana. The town of Rapalje, Montana, near Billings, was known as a timber and mining town. Sometime between 1919 and 1925, the Warrens moved again to Clark Fork, Idaho. Clark Fork was also a timber and mining boomtown.

Blanche and Russell Warren's wedding photo from 1915. Courtesy of the Warren family.

Children at the Quillayute School on Quillayute Prairie. This photo was taken in 1924 or 1925. The X over the boy's head in the left of the photo indicates a young Frank Warren. All that remains of this school today is the concrete and brink foundation resting in a field at Quillayute Prairie. Courtesy of the Warren family.

Left to right: Blanche Warren, (son) Charles Warren, (son) Frank Warren, Charles Sanger, Russell Warren, Alma Swiggim and Louise Alton (Allen), Florence Green, rest unknown. Photo was taken about 1921, in Clark Fork, Idaho. Courtesy of the Warren family.

Left to right: Blanche, Bertha, Russell, Frank, or Charles, unknown child, Elijah Taber with two grown daughters and one grandson. Taken about 1921 and courtesy of the Warren family.

Sometime around 1924 or 1925, the Warrens moved again to a logging camp near Forks, Washington, on the Quillayute Prairie. Quillayute Prairie was where the Quillayute Indian tribe lived before they moved to the present-day reservation at nearby La Push. The Quillayute people kept the prairie open with fire to encourage elk and deer to graze and promote wild berry production. The prairie is near the confluence of the Sol Duc and Bogachiel Rivers near La Push.

This was in the heyday of the logging industry in western Washington. The Olympic Peninsula contained some of the highest quality old-growth forest anywhere in the world. A great deal of money could be made exploiting these forests. Russell saw an opportunity to make money and took a job working for a local lumberman named Joe Leyendecker, cutting pulpwood on contract..

German-born Joseph Leyendecker and his wife, Ruth, arrived in western Washington about 1895 and settled with their nine children. The Warren family rented a cabin from Leyendecker. Today, this land is still owned by the Leyendecker family of Forks. The original Leyendecker homestead burned in about 1985, taking with it many family heirlooms and precious books.

In 2001, I had the pleasure of interviewing Russell Warren's cousin, Louise Allen. She described Russell as a hardworking, family-loving man. He paid his bills, took good care of his family and was not a drinker. He purchased a used 1927 Chevrolet two-door sedan. The previous owner reportedly lived in Port Angeles. In 1927, a new Chevy sedan would have sold for about $695. We don't know how much Russell paid for the car. However, even if he paid $500, that was still a lot of money in 1928 or 1929. A man was lucky to make $2000 a year in 1929.

A two-door Chevy sedan traveling west on the old Olympic Highway at Lake Crescent about 1928. Notice the gravel covered roadway and the wooden guardrail. The car is the same model as the one purchased by Russell Warren. It has the distinctive spare tire bracket holding the license plate. Courtesy of Olympic National Park.

5

THE MISSING ONES

On Wednesday July 3, 1929, Russell Warren left his cabin sometime around mid-morning to pick up his wife Blanche from the Lincoln Hospital in Port Angeles. The distance was about 60 miles. This was the last day Blanche and Russell Warren were to be seen alive. There are many questions about this trip that we may never find the answer. However, we can exploration of the facts as we know them.

The weather forecast for the Olympic Peninsula called for moderate northwest winds with a high temperature of 65 degrees, a low of 51 degrees and mostly clear skies. This was a typical day on the Olympic Peninsula in July.

In July on the Olympic Peninsula, the weather can be absolutely spectacular. For some reason, the sky over the Peninsula looks bluer than most skies in other areas of the United States. Although the area is known for its rainforests, it doesn't rain all the time. In fact, July, August, and September can be very warm and dry. Temperatures in the upper 80's and even the low 90's are not unusual. Even the humidity can be very low for extended periods of time. Wildfires in the summer months are very common in the Olympic Mountains, even in rainforest areas.

Why Blanche was in the hospital and for how long, we do not know. We could not locate hospital records from 1929. Investigators in 1929 apparently did not inquire as to the reason why she was hospitalized. However, Blanche could have been pregnant or was having difficulty with the pregnancy. She did lose a pregnancy several years prior which suggested that Blanche and Russell were still trying to have children. She did have a roommate while at the hospital that had undergone major surgery and was released about a week after Blanche. Her roommate was able to tell investigating deputies that Russell picked up Blanche from the Lincoln Hospital at 3:30 p.m. While there, Russell paid the hospital bill. The Lincoln Hospital was on the corner of Fourth and E streets in Port Angeles. The old hospital building was removed in 2010, after having been in poor condition for many years. It sat on a bluff overlooking the Port Angeles harbor and the local paper mill.

Investigators checking into the disappearance of the Warrens discovered that Russell drove to Port Angeles from his cabin on Quillayute Prairie on the morning of July 3. The drive would have taken him 2 to 3 hours at 20 to 25 miles per hour. One newspaper article stated that he left on July 2, but that is likely a mistake. He left his 2 sons, Charles and Frank, behind at Quillayute Prairie with neighbor friends and gave them his pocket watch and $35. Thirty-five dollars was a lot of money in 1929, especially for two young boys. That would be the equivalent of $600 in today's money. Did Russell have a premonition that he would not be returning? The Pockets watch and money must

This is the old Lincoln Hospital in Port Angeles in the year 2002. It was torn down in 2010. Blanche Warren stayed in this hospital the night before she disappeared. Courtesy of the author.

have raised the suspicion of the investigating deputy. Why would Russell give such a large amount of money and his pocket watch to his sons? Investigators must have thought that Russell may have had a plan not to return home on the night of July 3.

Russell also told his two sons that he would return with their mother so that they could all go to the Sol Duc Hot Springs the next day to celebrate the 4th of July. That particular statement, a somewhat strong statement, would lead one to believe he had every intention of returning to Quillayute Prairie that evening.

In 1929, investigators also discovered through interviews that while in Port Angeles, Russell bought a new washing machine for $60. He also paid a $100 grocery bill, a considerable sum of money for food in 1929. It is likely that he, like many people living in remote areas, bought several months of groceries and supplies when the opportunity presented itself.

Russell spent $100 on the grocery bill, $60 on the washing machine, paid the hospital bill (an unknown amount, but let's guess that the bill was $25 to $50), gave his sons $35, and paid the July and August mortgage on his car loan. He must have had somewhere in the neighborhood of $275 to $350 in his pocket before he left Quillayute Prairie. That was a very large sum of money for someone to be carrying around in 1929. Altogether, he spent a considerable amount of money while in Port Angeles.

Where does a man working in the forest cutting pulpwood acquire that kind of money? Russell was known as a very hard worker. Perhaps he was paid for completion of a logging contract and was flush with money, much like a gold miner who would come to town once every few months to spend his hard-earned cash. Perhaps the grocery bill was for the entire logging camp.

He placed the new washer and whatever groceries he was carrying in the back of the Chevy sedan. By removing the bottom part of the rear bench seat and folding the front driver and passenger seats completely forward, large objects like the washing machine could easily fit into the rear seat. The passenger and driver-side doors were easily wide enough to accommodate loading and unloading the washing machine.

Was the Lincoln Hospital the last stop of the day? Witnesses later came forward and reported to investigators that they had seen a car matching the description of the car Blanche and Russell were aboard at Lairds Corner, several miles west of Port Angeles, heading west on the Olympic Highway, apparently bound for home.

They were never seen again.

6

SHERIFF JACK PIKE

It was several days before friends of the Warrens reported to the Clallam County Sheriff's Department that Blanche and Russell did not return home to their sons as planned. On Tuesday, July 16 the *Port Angeles Evening News* displayed a front page headline:

"Man and Wife Are Missing; Boys Alone."

Why did it take nearly two weeks for the newspaper to report the disappearance? There was phone service from Forks to Port Angeles in 1929, so I think it was safe to say the phone must have been used to notify the authorities. The elected sheriff of Clallam County in 1929 was Jack Pike. Sheriff Pike was a man who we need to get to know a bit better, so that we can understand the reasoning behind some of his investigative efforts.

John "Jack" Pike was born on July 6, 1874, in Hazelock, New Zealand. He came to the United States in 1894 or 1895. He later found work at a shingle mill in Snoqualmie, Washington, where he met Sibyl Winters. She was working as a chambermaid at the Snoqualmie Lodge. They married on August 20, 1905, in Clallam County, Washington, while he was employed at the Filion Mill in Port Angeles. Sibyl Winters was from a pioneering family who had settled in the Morse Creek area in 1884, an area a few miles east of Port Angeles. The Pikes raised two daughters, Mary Ellen and Lillian, two sons, John and Robert, and an adopted son, Harry. Jack was a tall, lean man with bushy mustache and wavy hair. His granddaughter, Mary Ann Delong, described him as, "a quiet, thinking man with a postural characteristic of standing, leaning slightly forward, listening with his hands behind his back and his eyes intently on the speaker."

Jack, no doubt, had acquired considerable hunting and fishing skills while working in the largely forested area of the Olympic Peninsula where there were few stores and towns. He was an avid fisherman and must have been particularly pleased with the fishing at Lake Crescent.

Photo above left is of Jack Pike returning from a very successful fishing trip, taken some time in the 19230's, probably after fishing at Lake Crescent. Lake Crescent was known for its large Beardslee trout. To the right is Jack Pike in 1963 upon his return to Port Angeles for a visit. Courtesy of the Pike family.

Jack Pike was known to be very honest and kindhearted. In 1911, he was hired as the North Olympic Peninsula's first Game Warden. This was at a time when timber harvests were booming. The large population of elk on the Peninsula were extremely attractive to hunters and also vulnerable to poaching. Prior to 1911, there were not many game laws. The few game laws that were established were put into place by appointed game commissioners. There was essentially little or no enforcement of game laws. As the Olympic Peninsula population grew, and with the establishment of Mt. Olympus National Monument by President Roosevelt, it became apparent that something had to be done to protect one of the great natural resources of the Olympic Peninsula, the large Roosevelt elk population.

Jack Pike must have shown promise as a law enforcement office and must have been a very good Game Warden, popular with the citizens of Clallam County, because he was elected Sheriff of Clallam County in 1924. He had a reputation for tough enforcement of liquor prohibition laws and was credited with seizing 144 moonshine stills. In rural areas, the tax collector and the Game Warden are usually the most hated people in the county. Jack Pike served as Sheriff until 1930. After his six-year stint as Sheriff, he returned to his previous job as Game Warden. If he caught a poacher and determined that the meat was needed to feed a hungry family, he was known to suddenly turn completely blind. if he heard of a poacher bragging about killing game out of season or was killing wildlife commercially, he was known to be very tough and righteous and would spare the man no mercy.

In 1933, he accepted a job with the Port Angeles Police Department and retired as a lieutenant on July 1, 1950. In 1963, he came to Port Angeles to visit friends and was reportedly in possession of a black leather book which contained a record of hunting and trapping licenses and a journal of events dating back to 1913. The journal has not been seen since then.

One story in the diary tells of Chris Morgenroth, H. M. Fisher, Charles Stakemiller, Burnham Freeman, and Jack Pike releasing mountain goats at the base of Storm King Mountain at Rocky Point along the shores of Lake Crescent. The date was January 1, 1925 (prior to the establishment of Olympic National Park).

Jack Pike may have been one of the Peninsula's first true conservationists. He had a keen understanding of the importance of wildlife and the habitat that was needed to support it. He was known to have vigorously opposed the Elwha River dams construction project and wrote letters to the state commissioners in Olympia, Washington, expressing his opinion. When it was apparent the dams would be constructed, he strongly recommended that fish ladders be built so that the salmon runs of the Elwha River could continue. Most people back then, probably didn't even know what a fish ladder was. The fish ladders were not built, which resulted in nearly destroying one of the greatest salmon runs on the West Coast. It is entirely fitting the two dams that blocked the salmon runs on the Elwha River are being removed in an effort to restore the Elwha River salmon runs. I think Jack Pike would be very happy to know what is being done on the Elwha River. Jack Pike died on September 30, 1968, at the age of 94 and was living in Reedsport, Oregon, with his daughter at the time of his death.

In November 2001, I made an inquiry with the Clallam County Sheriff's Department asking to search for case records and reports from the 1920s that Jack Pike may have written relating to the Warren disappearance. Unfortunately, case files from that era were destroyed many years prior to my inquiry. For me, to piece this case and story together, I had to rely on newspaper articles and stories told by the descendants of the Warrens.

Sheriff Jack Pike along with Deputies Harvey McNeil, Alex Kemp, James Gallagher, and Washington State Patrol Officer Howard Tull were assigned to the Warren investigation. Ed Brooks a well-known Lake Crescent resident and pioneer homesteader assisted the officers with the investigation.

We don't really know if Sheriff Pike actually took the lead with the Warren investigation or if he assigned the bulk of the sleuthing to his deputies. I tend to believe that he was very much involved in the case, from conducting interviews to collecting evidence. Pike was at the height of his law enforcement career, perhaps the best man to lead the investigation. The pattern and methodology used in the case matched his style. He was tenacious and determined. I believe his officers drove to Forks within the next day or a few days after July 4, and interviewed the Warren boys, Frank (age 14) and Charles (age 12) at the rented cabin on Quillayute Prairie. If Sheriff Pike was there, he would have sensed the fear, anxiety and great sense of loss the boys felt over the disappearance of their parents.

Sheriff Pike was known for being an inquisitive person. He was sensitive to other people's feeling and a good listener. The strange disappearance of the Warren parents would have piqued his keen police instincts. For these reasons, I don't think he was at that first interview with the boys. His deputies must have briefed him when they returned e and told him that the Warrens were probably away for a few days and that a missing person investigation was not warranted just yet. The boys, being in possession of $35 and their father's pocket watch, must have led the interviewing deputies to believe that Blanche and Russell Warren were visiting relatives or friends.

Charles and Frank, told the deputies their father had left on July 3, with the promise that both parents would return to take them to the Sol Duc Hot Springs for a July the Fourth holiday celebration. This would be something two young boys living in a small cabin would not forget easily. The boys would have also told the deputies that their father had gone to the hospital in Port Angeles to pick up their mother.

This bit of information led Sheriff Pike's deputies to the Lincoln Hospital in Port Angeles, where they were able to interview the hospital roommate of Blanche Warren, Mrs. K. E. Rudolph living at 402

North Eunice Street in Port Angeles. Mrs. Rudolph told Sheriff Pike's deputies that Russell Warren had come to the hospital and left with his wife and luggage at approximately 3:30 p.m. on July 3. Mrs. Rudolph was later released from the hospital on July 10 and had reportedly been recovering from a major operation. Patient and financial records from the Lincoln Hospital from the late 1920s were destroyed long ago when the hospital was converted to a home. These records could have told what ailment was affecting Blanche Warren, requiring her hospitalization.

The Sheriff's Department set themselves hard at work, trying to locate relatives of the missing couple. The investigators discovered that Russell and Blanche were from Wisconsin and had relatives in Heron, Montana. A "tracer" was sent out to Heron to find out if the couple had gone there. They reportedly had gone to Heron where Blanche's mother and grandmother lived, for a short visit two years before but supposedly told the boys they were going and had left the them in the care of neighbors.

Nearly two weeks went by without much news as to the progress of the investigation. Sheriff Pike's deputies must have been waiting for responses from parents and family in Idaho and Montana. The Sheriff's Department likely did not contact the newspapers, thinking that the case would soon be solved.

In the days following the disappearance, young Charles and Frank remained at Quillayute Prairie. They must have been quite frantic and upset over their missing parents. Family friends were caring for them and they were probably not in school due to the summer break. The boys must have had a great sense of urgency to know what had happened to their parents and must have felt the pity of the community over their loss. The boys must have known, perhaps as early as July 4, that something tragic must have happened, because even though the deputies were not convinced, the boys knew that their parents would not have abandoned them, that their parents would have done everything possible to come back home and to make good on the promise to take them to the Sol Duc Hot Springs.

The first newspaper article of the Warren disappearance showed up on the front page of the *Port Angeles Evening News* on Tuesday, July 16, 1929. It had now been thirteen days since the couple disappeared. This is the first article to appear in the local newspapers alerting the public the Warrens had disappeared.

Newspaper article from the *Port Angeles Evening News* dated July 16, 1929. This was the first newspaper article about the disappearance of Mr. and Mrs. Warren. It states the Warrens two sons are *"anxiously waiting the return of their parents."* Courtesy of the Clallam County Historical Society.

Sheriff Pike's deputies must have gotten negative responses from the "tracers" sent to relatives. With no witnesses and few leads to follow, the logical step would have been to seek assistance from the public to for information that would lead to the discovery of the Blanche and Russell Warren and their car. The investigators used the right tactic, although a bit late, to contact the newspaper and have the story well publicized with front page articles. Someone must have seen something!

For the Clallam County Sheriff's Department, the investigation had gotten off to a slow start compared to today's missing person cases. In 1929, communication technology included radio, newspapers, telegrams, and an emerging telephone system. There was no television, no cell phones, texting, no Internet or computers, no fax machines, no instant messaging, and no two-way radio systems for the law enforcement officers to talk to each other. Communicating with the public was by radio and newspaper. Communicating with each other was done largely by meeting face to face or talking on the phone when there was one available.

After two weeks with no word of their parent's whereabouts, the Warren boys must have begun to fear the worst. They probably felt very apprehensive when approached by a stranger or a uniformed police officer who might bring the chilling news that their parents were found dead. Sadly, however, the boys never received this news in their lifetimes.

Over the next two weeks, investigators would interview several people who had reportedly witnessed an incident or heard something. Newspaper articles seemed to be generating interest and concern in the community. Could a potential clue be uncovered? In a *Port Angeles Evening News* article dated July 30, the reporter misspelled the Warren's last name, spelling it Warner.

"Mr. and Mrs. Warner Are Not Yet Located"

After a month without their parents, the Warren boys were reportedly frantic for their return. At the end of July , Deputies discovered that Blanches mother, Bertha Matteson, was working in a hotel in Spokane Washington They contacted her and made her aware of the investigation surrounding her missing daughter. Once she learned of the investigation, it is unknown if she traveled to Port Angeles, but I suspect that she did. It was a one day train ride from Spokane to Seattle. As August began, there was a greater effort by the Sheriff's Department to find the Warrens, and I think it was because Blanche's mother or a family member had expressed an urgency to find Blanche and Russell. Blanche's mother wrote several letters to her family members in Montana and Idaho, telling them of the progress of the investigation.

The two boys were in the care of Mr. and Mrs. Ed Marsh at

Quillayute Prairie. The newspaper articles probably generated local interest and gossip, especially at the Singer Tavern, along the shores of Lake Crescent, where many tourists would stop. Sheriff Pike was a very wise to use the media to ask for help from the local community to locate a missing couple. Local travelers and tourists must have read the newspaper articles and were aware of the investigation.

At the beginning of August, rumors began circulating in Forks, Lake Crescent and Port Angeles. *An automobile containing a young couple that had plunged into Lake Crescent while traveling along the Olympic Highway.* Washington State Highway Patrolman Howard Tull, working with Sheriff Pike and his men, heard the rumors and tried to find the source or person who may have seen the accident at Lake Crescent. According to newspaper accounts, the rumor was started when a sailor, stationed on one of the battleships in the Port Angeles Harbor over the Fourth of July, reported to local people that he saw an automobile leave the roadway and plunge into Lake Crescent about the time of the disappearance of the Warrens. The sailor said the accident happened near Fairholm (the west end of the lake).

Patrolman Tull and the Sherriff's Deputies discovered that the battleships stationed at the Port Angeles Harbor in July had left and was now moored in Seattle. Patrolman Tull needed to find the sailor to get a firsthand account of the rumored accident. Patrolman Tull contacted the *Port Angeles Evening News* requesting an article be written to ask citizens for any information about the rumors or the disappearance and to contact him. Interestingly, the name of the Warrens was misspelled again as *Warner* in the newspaper article, perhaps because Patrolman Tull was providing the information. Maybe, Patrolman Tull wasn't working with the sheriff's deputies as closely as we thought . . .

The newspaper account is dated Saturday, August 3, 1929.

"Tragedy Rumor Being Traced"

On Monday, August 5th, the newspaper finally got the spelling of the Warrens correct for the first time since July 16. By now, there was enough information and public interest in the story that it was necessary to make sure the spelling was correct. Over the weekend of August 3 and 4, Sheriff Pike and his men began focusing their efforts on the shores of Lake Crescent, searching for clues as to where a car may have left the roadway and in an attempt to verify the rumors. As of Sunday evening, August 4, the Sheriff's Department and the State Road Crew who worked and traveled the road each day had not found or reported evidence of an accident scene. It had now been over a month since the accident had taken place, and the clues, if they were visible from the roadway would be subtle at best. The sun, wind, waves, and rain would quickly erase clues on the shore. It would take a sharp eye to spot things that should not be there or just do not look natural. People who used the lake often, such as fisherman or the ferryboat operators, would be good candidates to search the lakeshore.

Early in the week of August 5, Patrolman Tull traveled to the Port of Seattle and found the sailor who was the source of the rumors. The sailor was identified as Curtis Thompson, stationed aboard the battleship Tennessee. According to his initial statement, he had seen a car plunge into the water at Lake Crescent. Patrolman Tull convinced him to return to Lake Crescent so that they could pinpoint the location where he saw the vehicle leave the roadway and plunge into the lake. Thompson told Patrolman Tull that he believed the accident took place on Sunday, July 14 and not July 3. Thompson said that he was driving five men who were loggers to Beaver (ten miles west of Lake Crescent) and saw a roadster traveling as a high rate of speed one half mile west of Singer Tavern (Barnes Point), *"swerve in loose gravel and plunge into Lake Crescent at the first curve beyond Barnes Point. We stopped and watched bubbles came to the surface. Two other cars stopped, one was an Oakland sedan. After a time, we drove on thinking others would report it. On my return to Port Angeles, I mentioned the fact to several friends, but they only told me I was spinning a yarn."* Thompson told Patrolman Tull and Sheriff Pike that he believed the date was July 14, because that was the day of a sailing regatta on Lake Sutherland (a lake one mile east of Lake Crescent).

Could there have been two vehicle accidents at Lake Crescent? Could this be a coincidence? Sheriff Pike was starting to believe there may be, in fact, two vehicles in the lake. Thompson's statement, especially the date of July 14, gave his claim a whole lot less credibility and weight with regard to solving the Warren case. However, the Thompson's story was creditable enough to suggest that a second car was in the lake and needed to be investigated completely. Investigators knew the car the Warrens were in was a small sedan and not a roadster and also knew the date of the Warren disappearance to be July 3. The date of July 3 for the disappearance of the Warrens was taken with high reliability. The Thompson account of an accident at Lake Crescent seemed to be highly inconsistent with the Warren case. Nonetheless, there was an outside possibility it could be related to the disappearance of Blanche and Russell Warren. This definitely needed to be investigated.

On Wednesday morning, August 7, Sheriff Pike and his deputies, along with Patrolman Tull, were at Lake Crescent with Thompson, dragging the lake bottom from a rowboat. Sheriff Pike and his men were able to see down into the lake many feet and reported, "*Marks on brush where the beach shelved off convinces me that a car went into the lake. No evidence of a car leaving the road is apparent from shoreline except several bits of broken roadway. But when we rowed out from shore and looked into the clear water, we could see where brush under the water had been broken in two places. The men were able to catch something with the grappling hook, and the team got excited, thinking they may have hooked the car. It turned out to be the top of a submerged tree, of which there are many in the lake.*"

On Friday, August 9, Sheriff Pike, his deputies, and Patrolman Tull were convinced that at least one vehicle, if not two vehicles, were at the bottom of Lake Crescent. Convinced Thompson's story was accurate, Sheriff Pike, together with County Prosecuting Attorney John Wilson, asked Commander Ferguson of the Navy vessels stationed in the Port Angeles Harbor for divers and equipment so that a underwater search one mile west of Singer Tavern could be made. Their efforts were thwarted however when he was told that the ships were scheduled to leave the harbor that very day, Friday, August 9. The dive gear Sheriff Pike was asking for would be needed the next day, a Saturday, August 10 or possibly Sunday, August 11, the team of investigators could secure a barge-style vessel to use as a dive platform.

When it was learned that divers and gear from the navy ships would not be available, Frank Mapes, a trained diver and former employee of the Finch Deep Sea Diving Company of Seattle, came forward to volunteer his services.

Dive gear for this effort would be primitive by today's standards. Self-contained underwater breathing apparatus, or scuba, would be many years away as a viable tool for diving and searching underwater. A dive operation in 1929, in fresh or salt water would have gone something like this: The diver would have been dressed in a suit of heavy, waterproof canvas impregnated and sealed with rubber, fitted with a thick, rubber-necked collar. A brass helmet that weighed about forty pounds was fitted onto the rubber collar to make a watertight seal. Air hoses would be mounted to a valve on the helmet. The helmet was built with four viewing ports so the diver could look straight ahead, left, right, and overhead. Looking at one's feet would be a problem and likely result in the diver rolling over in the water. The diver wore heavy lead shoes for weight to compensate for the flotation of the suit. The whole suit weighed about one hundred pounds. Air was provided from the surface by the hoses attached to a hand-operated air compressor that had a hand crank. The diver would be able to walk around on the bottom of the lake or ocean, if it was not too steep, muddy, or treacherous. The diver could not swim and had a very delicate balance point. If current or reduced water visibility was present, that complicated the dive even more. The diver could only communicate by pulling on the rope that was used to lower and raise him.

A large platform, barge or boat was used to support the team, diver, hose and compressor. This type of diving did not have a dive partner. The diver, once having left the support vessel, was alone with a very limited ability to communicate any serious problems. There was no way for the diver to bail out and rescue himself. The diver was at the mercy of the surface support team. The surface support team needed to be well-trained.

Sheriff Pike saw that the lake "*shelved off abruptly*" near shore, but he was told by one of the Lake Crescent pioneers, probably Ed Brooks, that "*The shelve (sic) was not very deep and a level area would be founded (sic) a short distance out.*" Other locals told Sheriff Pike that the shelf continued downward for a long distance. A local newspaper article explained that "*a steam shovel which left the Port Angeles Western Railroad was raised several years ago and went nearly halfway across the Narrows of Lake Crescent underwater.*"

On Saturday, August 10, unable to acquire Navy dive gear, Sheriff Pike located dive gear from Finch Deep Sea Diving Company. Henry and crew are pictured on the next page. R. R. Blain, a company employee, drove the gear from Seattle to Port Angeles, arriving at 6:30 a.m. Port Angeles fireman Ernest Harding, took the gear in a city truck to the Lake. Blain was in charge of the dive operation and fitted Mapes to the dive suit, rigged the air compressor and fitted the hoses to his helmet. Local Lake expert, Ed Brooks towed a small float to the scene to act as a support vessel for the operation.

Other support people were Patrolman Howard Tull, Deputies Harvey McNeill, James Gallagher and Willis Smith, a commercial diver from San Diego. He was visiting friends in the area and volunteered his services. The equipment was set up on the small platform which was equipped with a strong ladder to assist the very heavy diver with access to the water. Frank Mapes began his dive at 11:09 a.m. and descended to a depth of 50 feet landing on "*a mountain of shale rock under water*". Mapes was able to make it to a depth of 78 feet before running out of air hose. He was back at the surface at 11:21 a.m., a 12 minute dive.

A 1920's era photo of the Finch Commercial Diving Company working at a job site on Lake Washington near Seattle Washington. Note the heavy dive suits and support barge. Courtesy of the Finch family.

He reported to Sheriff Pike that, *"There is a mountain of shale down there into which the car may have plunged and covered itself by now. And even if it is not covered up, the dragging operation would only tend to pull dead trees and shale rock over it."* The dive location was probably the area just west of Barnes Point where the road closely abuts the water edge. Today, this spot would be close to Milepost 226 of Highway 101, the first location east of Barnes Point where the roadway is very close to the shoreline.

Mapes reported to Sheriff Pike and the Port Angeles Evening News, as their support team was unscrewing the helmet, *"There's a huge channel through a mountain of shale down there, showing plain as day that an object the size of an automobile plowed for a long distance through it recently. It looks like a yarder had yanked a giant log through loose earth— I am sure it is the path of an automobile."* This may have been the path created by the log hooked and dragged by Sheriff Pike's team the previous Wednesday.

Sheriff Pike took this statement as a positive sign, believing that they were searching the right area. Sheriff Pike ordered a sounding and dragging operation (sounding is the act of measuring the depth of water with a weighted line.) He fixed a line from the shore to the point where Mapes had turned back thinking that this was the line of travel of the car. About one hundred people stood on the shore, watching the dive operation take place, which must have been a great source of entertainment and curiosity. Franks Mapes' wife was in the crowd and was said to be very relieved when her husband was safely on the surface.

Later on this day, Sheriff Pike interviewed a friend of Russell Warren, a man named Cliff Wilson. Wilson stated he talked to Russell the night before he went to Port Angeles (July 2nd). Russell told Cliff he had fallen asleep at the wheel while driving on a previous visit to the hospital. Wilson went on to say that Russell awakened just in time to find his car was cross-wise on the road, heading for the lake. Russell stopped his auto, went down to the lake, and bathed his hands and face before proceeding on the trip. *"He had been working late,"* Wilson said. Wilson further stated, *"They certainly were planning to come back, because the last thing Warren said to me was that he had to be back to Bogachiel by July 4, because he promised the kids they would spend the day at the Sol Duc Hot Springs."* Wilson said that Russell also promised Joe Leyendecker to start on the pulp wood work again on July 5 or 6, as the work was behind.

On Sunday, August 11, Sheriff Pike's deputies, Harvey McNeill and James Gallagher, along with Ed Brooks sounded the area lined out by Sheriff Pike in hopes of hooking the car. They did not find anything to report.

All in all, it was a very busy week for the investigators. Sheriff Pike gave considerable thought to the witness statement the sailor Curtis Thompson, had given him. Thompson felt sure that the day he witnessed the accident was July 14, a Sunday. The large discrepancy between that July 14 and July 3, the day Pike clearly believed the couple disappeared, was hard to reconcile. Thompson had apparently witnessed an accident of some type and within the month prior to July 14.

Sheriff Pike interviewed Curtis Thompson's parents, who owned a cabin on Lake Sutherland where the regatta had taken place. Thompson's parents stated their son was in the Lake Crescent area on July 7th. This undermined his story and demonstrated that Thompson was unable to accurately fix the date he saw the accident. Sheriff Pike now put forth Sunday, July 7, as the date Thompson had witnessed an accident.

With very thin physical evidence to work with and a now unreliable eye witness, the mystery seemed even cloudier. Where were the Warrens from Wednesday July 3rd to Sunday July 7th? Why had they not returned home to their children?

Evidence seen by diver Mapes should have been more significant. Thompson stated he and the other witnesses saw bubbles coming to the surface where the roadster disappeared into the lake. They did not report any items such as clothing, bottles, even fuel, floating on the water. They did not report any skid marks or slide marks on the road or edge of the road, and none were apparently visible one month later. Sheriff Pike had not received any reports of missing persons in the area other than the Warrens.

A few days later, Sheriff Pike heard another rumor which appeared to be consistent with Thompson's statement. The unnamed source, a dry cleaning service driver, apparently also saw an accident on July 14, and gave the same version as Thompson, except that he said the automobile was a sedan rather than a roadster.

Harry LeGear, the superintendent of the Port Angeles Western Railroad (the railroad that hauled timber from the forests of the Olympic Peninsula during World War I), offered Sheriff Pike the use of a huge magnet that could be tethered and dropped into the lake. The same magnet was used several years prior to 1929 to locate a previously mentioned steam shovel that was part of the railroad company's equipment which and which was affixed to a railcar. The steam shovel had gone into the lake from the north shore side of the lake. The shovel was located halfway between the north and south sides of the lake in the Narrows.

On Monday, August 12, Mrs. Ross Bolt reported to the Chelan County Sheriff (in eastern Washington State) that she saw what appeared to be fresh graves at the Leyendecker farm, near the Warren home. Sheriff Pike received the information and learned that Mrs. Ross had camped near the Warren cabin the previous week. Clallam County Prosecuting Attorney, John M. Wilson, visited the Leyendecker farm several days later and discovered that the "fresh grave" was a pile of roots dug up from the garden. On Tuesday, August 13, Russell's son, Frank, read a newspaper account of the "fresh grave" and told Sheriff Pike the grave contained a dead cow that he and his brother had helped Joe Leyendecker bury weeks earlier.

The two boys, Charles and Frank, were now in the care of Mr. and Mrs. Fred Meyers and Mrs. Ed Marsh and had been given a cabin of their own. The boys reportedly were hopeful that at some point, their parents would return. Rumors were that when someone would come to the cabin, they would drop whatever they were doing and rush to the door, hoping that it would be their parents. The Meyers told the local newspaper that the boys were well-behaved and had won the hearts of the Meyers. Fred Meyers stated that Russell Warren had come to his store near Forks, Washington, on June 30 to purchase a few things. Meyers stated, *"Warren was always a good man to pay his bills, was a hard worker, and had plenty of work ahead of him on the river."* Young Frank had been reading the newspapers and was following the investigation. Frank told Mr. Meyers that he believed that his parents were in the car that supposedly went into Lake Crescent, as witnessed by Curtis Thompson.

On Tuesday, August 13, Sheriff Pike and his men dragged the Lake bottom with grappling hooks, the same area identified by Curtis Thompson, to a depth of 110 feet. At the 78 feet, the level reached by diver Frank Mapes, Deputy Gallagher found that the lake dropped off abruptly. They found no additional clues.

Sheriff Pike and his men had done nearly all they could to find the car and solve the disappearance of the Warrens. All clues had been investigated and had been explained. Without new evidence or clues, the case seems to have come to a halt. At this point, Sheriff Pike was ready to suspend the search at Lake Crescent due to the lack of creditable evidence.

During the week of August 12, Sheriff Pike received a letter from Mrs. W. C. Saleber of Bellingham, Washington. Mrs. Saleber was apparently a close, personal friend of the Warrens and relayed the family history of the Warrens. Mrs. Saleber told Sheriff Pike that she had written a letter to the them recently, and it had gone unanswered. She told Sheriff Pike that the Warrens had visited her home in Clarks Fork, Idaho the previous summer. The Warrens came from Warren, Wisconsin, named after the Warren family. Relatives still lived in Warren, Wisconsin, and nearby towns. Sheriff Pike received a list of the relatives and sent tracers to them.

On Wednesday, August 14, Sheriff Pike and the newspaper received many telephone calls from citizens who wanted to know more about the rumor that four bodies had been pulled from Lake Crescent. Apparently, a local citizen, known to tell a few wild stories had been spreading the tale. There was no truth to the rumor whatsoever.

The two Warren boys having read these exaggerated stories, by now must have been grief stricken. To constantly hear rumors and innuendoes must have been difficult for them. They obviously loved their parents and missed them dearly. For them to not have a resolution to the disappearance of their parents was perhaps worse than having to deal with seeing their bodies. The boys wanted to know what happened to their parents!

On Friday, August 16, Sheriff Pike heard from Blanche Warren's mother, Bertha Matteson, living in Spokane, Washington, that she was coming to Port Angeles.

With the search for the Warrens at Lake Crescent all but closed, brothers Harry and Ed Brooks must have thought that there had to be evidence someplace along the lakeshore. But if not at the area described by Curtis Thompson, where? A systematic search of the lakeshore from a boat might reveal clues that would not be seen from land. Thus far, now six weeks since the disappearance of the Warrens, no such search of the south shore of the lake had been done, especially where the road is close to the water's edge and unprotected by trees or guardrail.

Ed and Harry, who had been living on the lake for many years, were perhaps the most knowledgeable people with regard to the lake and local roads and understood the its many hidden characteristics. On Friday, August 16, Harry Brooks was out scouting the south shore about 1.5 miles east of the west end, near a prominent point of land that jutted out into the lake. He found what appeared to be evidence that an automobile had left the roadway and had crashed into a cedar log near the shoreline, tearing limbs from the log. There was broken glass that seemed to be from a windshield and what appeared to be tire impressions. This area is a full three miles further west and on the same south side of the lake as the area described by Curtis Thompson. The road at this location was not protected by a wooden guardrail, which existed in a few other dangerous locations along the lake. The road surface was one or two feet above the lake level and only a few feet from the shore of the lake. Just 20 feet out from shore, the lake was already over 60 feet deep and dropped quickly into the dark blue of the water. Upon returning to his cabin, he immediately notified Sheriff Pike of his discovery.

Sheriff Pike drove to the scene the next morning, Saturday August 17, and found the evidence that he had been hoping for. He saw clear evidence that a vehicle had indeed rolled off the roadway and had fallen into deep water. Sheriff Pike described the location as *"a little curve in the highway."* The road was several feet above the lakeshore. A cedar log was on the *"shelving side of the road bed."* Sheriff Pike saw evidence that an automobile traveling west got too near the edge of the road and rolled down to the side of the bank, striking a cedar log, tearing away many small limbs, shattering the windshield, and deposited glass in the shallows. The glass appeared to have been in the water for several weeks. For the car to break the windshield on the cedar log, the car would have had to roll over. However, the windshield could have been broken by objects inside the car sliding forward (such as a washing machine) as the vehicle quickly came to a stop when it hit the cedar tree and water. Blanche and Russell Warren were likely in the path of these moving objects.

This was new evidence, new clues, and new hope for Sheriff Pike to solve the disappearance of the Warrens. He probably had a strong feeling that Harry Brooks found the exact spot where the Warrens had disappeared.

On Sunday, August 18, the investigative team began a new sounding and dragging operation with hopes of hooking on to a 1927 Chevy sedan. They named the newly discovered site Madrona Point, after a large, old and overhanging Madrona trees near the shore . The dragging operation was conducted to a depth of one hundred feet. Larger pieces of windshield glass were retrieved from the shore and shallow water and transported into Port Angeles. At the Chevy dealership in Port Angeles, Joseph Parts (that was his real name) examined the glass and told Pike that the glass was not the kind of glass used in Chevrolet automobiles. However, Sheriff Pike took this bit of evidence with a certain amount of skepticism.

Sheriff Pike described the near-shoreline area as being a shelf a few feet wide and with the lake bottom dropping off to an *"undetermined depth where the water is a deep blue and the bottom cannot be seen."* Based on this description, the evidence suggested a car failed to negotiate the *"little curve in the highway"* and headed straight into the lake. Could it be that Russell had fallen asleep again while driving and drifted off the right side of the road?

On Monday, August 19, the investigative team continued to search in the area of Madrona Point, dragging a hook to a depth of 100 feet. Deputies McNeill and Gallagher found a sun visor at a depth of 40 feet near the first ledge. They were able to see the visor from the surface due to the extremely clear water and smooth surface. The searchers may have been aided by a window box used to peer into the depths of the lake from the surface; much like a snorkel swimmer would use a dive mask. They used a small hook and line to snag the visor and bring it to the surface. It was the only piece of evidence to come to the surface on that day. It was described as leather, with the screws still in it, suggesting that the visor was, as Sheriff Pike described in a newspaper account, *"torn from the automobile as it turned over on the first rocky ledge after plunging into the lake."* The visor was transported to Port Angeles by Pike who, the next day, took it to Joseph Parts at the local Chevy dealership. He identified it as like those used in Chevrolet cars.

The Sheriff stated in another newspaper story, *"The Warrens are in Lake Crescent. A man that paid the hospital bill, paid $100 on a grocery bill, and made two months payment on his automobile, and bought a washing machine for his wife certainly wasn't contemplating running away. It is injustice to the children to even indicate that Russell ran away, for all evidence points to the fact the family was closely attached and that the reason for leaving the hospital on July 3 was to return to the Bogachiel River and take the boys to the Hot Springs for the Fourth of July. They were seen at Laird's Corner, westbound, on the afternoon of July 3. Their journey ended when their car leaped into the lake at Madrona Point."*

Sheriff Pike appeared to have great compassion for the two boys, having met them several times by now. When they heard by telephone the news that the deputies had found evidence at a new location along the lake, and had found evidence including a Chevy automobile sun visor, they were reportedly *"electrified."*

The next problem the investigative team had was to figure out how to search very deep water in near vertical underwater terrain. This type of terrain would leave little or no footing for a diver. Sheriff Pike had already spent a considerable sum of money from his annual county budget to find the Warrens. He stated the next logical step was to bring in a large scow, a diver, and raising apparatus. The cost of such an operation was beyond the means of the sheriff's department budget. Sheriff Pike would have to ask the Clallam County Commissioners to approve extra funding to support this operation.

On Tuesday morning, August 27, a special session of the Clallam County commissioners authorized Sheriff Pike to hire a diver to search for the Chevrolet sedan and solve the mystery of the disappearance of the Warrens once and for all. The commissioners had visited the site of the search the previous day with Sheriff Pike, and while looking into the crystal clear water, one of the commissioners saw a shiny flower vase, described as the type typically used in automobiles. They were able to fish it out. The next day, the vase was shown to the former owner of the 1927 Chevy sedan the Warrens were driving. He confirmed the vase looked like one he had placed in the car on the inside door post when he was the owner.

Commissioner George Lamb stated, *"Enough evidence has been secured to warrant the expenditures of a reasonable amount of money in an attempt to find the bodies of Mr. and Mrs. Russell Warren. The finding of marks in the lake bank showing a path of an automobile, the discovery of the visor to the car, and lastly the vase from the lost car make almost conclusive evidence that the car and bodies of the lost people are in Lake Crescent near Fairholm, and we will authorize Sheriff Pike to do everything possible to find them."*

That day, having now found a new source of funds to continue the investigation as well as new evidence, traveled to Seattle to negotiate with Finch Deep Sea Diving Company. They were a commercial diving company well-known in the Seattle area for successful underwater searches and construction projects. The desire was to have them come to

Lake Crescent to find the 1927 Chevy and hopefully find the Warrens.

On this same day, Tuesday, August 27, Bertha Matteson arrived in Port Angeles, traveling from Spokane where she had been living for several months. She met and was briefed on the situation by County Prosecuting Attorney John M. Wilson and sheriff's deputies since Sheriff Pike went to Seattle to meet with the divers he was hiring. She must have heard the news of compelling evidence having been found and that perhaps a conclusion to the investigation was near. She also must have prepared herself with the inevitability that she would have to bury her daughter and son-in-law, resigning herself to the fact that six weeks had passed and the missing loved ones were almost certainly dead. Only a miracle would bring them back alive. Bertha writes, *"Have to go to Port Angeles Monday to the boys. No word has been found of the missing ones. Boys most frantic (sic). Have done all I can from here. Did not have money to go on . . ."*

The next day, Mrs. Matteson left Port Angeles and traveled to Forks, to the home of Mr. and Mrs. Edward March who were caring for the boys. Bertha probably rode by the very spot near the water on the Olympic Highway where her daughter had disappeared. Her mission was to retrieve her two grandsons and take them back to Heron, Montana, where she could care for them. She had heard a story that the previous search team had found a car buried in shale and had attempted to bring it to the surface from 75 feet of water. The facts were a little off and were surely related to the tree the search team had hooked near Singer Tavern over one month earlier.

Above and on the following page, are an envelope and letter from Blanche's mother, Bertha Matteson to her family members, dated August 23, 1929. They were in the possession of Louise Alton Allen in 2001, when I interviewed her at her home in Port Angeles. Courtesy of the Warren family.

I will write you when I find
out more I shall bring boys
home and do my best.
I have been under Drs care
over a week but dont tell Vern
I will be better when I get there
This Suspense is killing me,
why is such any lot I cant see
but I must not murmur,
God must be right in his ways,
careing for us. so his will be done
not ours, let me know how mother
is at Mrs. E Marsh, Quillayute Tavern
and also at Spokane Wash. Wash,
Lbel, so if I dont I get one will the other General
Please dont wait so long as there
are many of you so some me now
surely write me, I must know, to
Help hold one up for what I have to
go through dont let it come a shock
to one girls Please, now I must close,
love to each one and Pray I may
Have strenth to Keep up. your sister
                          Bertha Mattson

After Sheriff Pike returned from Seattle, he and his men spent the day on Wednesday getting together the necessary support equipment to assist the dive operation now scheduled for Thursday, August 29. This would include a wooden scow, which is a square-shaped flat-bottomed boat. The diving equipment, air pump and support staff would have weighed a considerable sum requiring a craft of considerable width and length. The scow needed to be large enough to also support a derrick and winch to raise the car should it be found. Fortunately, there were several barges and boats around the lake that could support such an operation. There were several still usable and built before the Olympic Highway opened in 1922. These barges were used to transport vehicles, wagons, and horses from each end of the lake..

On the morning and afternoon of Thursday, August 29, R. R. Blain of the Finch Deep Sea Diving Company, started a study of the lake bottom terrain to determine what he would encounter as a diver. Using a sounding device (most likely a thick rope or cable and weighted steel hook marked with depth readings) he found that the lake was about 350 feet deep at a distance of 400 feet from shore. He was able to locate where the steep drop offs were in relation to where the car likely fell into the lake. While conducting the survey, he hoped to be able to hook the car with the sounding gear and raise the vehicle to the surface. R. R. Blaine reported to the newspaper that his company had conducted a similar operation in Lake Washington near Seattle by recovering a heavy truck from 348 feet of water.

This Lake Crescent dragging operation was going to be a extensive and technical operation. Blaine used a 750-foot hawser (thick rope), 150 feet of cable, a wooden cask and several anchors. The effort was conducted using the old ferryboat Arcadia, operated by Julius Peterson as well as a large scow. During the dragging operation that day, the crew managed to snag a large 200 foot tree and raised it to the surface. The tree was reportedly solid and showed no evidence of being rotten after having been in the lake for many years. The tree was smooth and had no limbs. To release the tree from the dragging tackle, Deputy

Harvey McNeil had to chop it free with an axe and noted the chips cut from the tree sank to the bottom as if they were stone. This was obviously a very old tree and had been in the depths of the lake for a very long time, preserved by very cold and clean water. The tree was towed out toward the middle of the lake and returned to the depths of the lake. Blaine was confident that the method he was using would snag the car and that they would be able to raise it to the surface using the windlass (a winch). The operation must have been difficult, given the challenging underwater terrain, cliffs, large rocks, and the other obstacles on the bottom.

The description of the operation and the width of the sweep suggest the search team should have snagged the Warren's 1927 Chevy sedan. However, they would have had to snag a strong section of the car frame to raise it; for as we later learned, Chevy sedans from that period had door frames and upper structures made of wood with sheet-metal paneling. A hook may not have held and could have torn through the structure of the car.

For whatever reasons, the Warrens or their car were not to be found by these hard working and dedicated men. Once again, Sheriff Pike and his team failed in their quest. They were however, successful in finding evidence that the car and the Warrens were in Lake Crescent. It was almost as if there were forces at play that denied the search team the satisfaction of finding the car and recovering the bodies. Knowing what we know today, Sheriff Pike and his men should have found the car using their search methods but they simply did not. Bad luck?

By now, the Finch Deep Sea Diving Company had been at Lake Crescent for two days and had failed to retrieve the Warrens' car or their bodies. All the available technology of 1929 had been tried without success. It must have been extremely frustrating to know that the Warrens' auto was beneath the surface of the lake, probably directly under their vessels, in a rather small geographic area, but yet it could not be found. For a second time, Sheriff Pike and his team were out of luck, out of money, and out of patience. They had given it their best shot, and they came up short.

All the while, Blanche Warren's mother, Bertha Matteson, was in Port Angeles with the two boys, waiting for the results of the search at Lake Crescent. However, the news was not good: nothing had been found.

It had now been over eight weeks since the disappearance of the Warrens, and significant clues had been found. However, the two biggest clues, the car and the bodies of Blanche and Russell Warren, had not been found. Sheriff Pike was charged with the difficult task of telling Blanche's mother that the search effort was over and that Blanche and Russell were somewhere in the lake, out of reach of the search team. Blanche's mother and the two boys would leave Port Angeles without closure, without ever knowing for sure what happened.

On that Tuesday Blanche's mother made plans to leave by the weekend to travel back to Montana. Her plan was postponed when she discovered that there were certain important business papers, such as contracts and receipts, missing from the Warren cabin on Quillayute Prairie. They were needed to close out accounts, settle debts and other family business in Port Angeles and Forks. Her wish to have the papers returned was reported in the September 3 edition of the Port Angeles Evening News. In the article, she also thanked the generous people who took her grandsons in, while the search was in progress, feeding, housing, clothing the boys, and looking after their needs.

At the weekly Clallam County Commissioners' meeting on Tuesday evening, the Commissioners authorized Sheriff Pike to offer a $250 reward to anyone who could provide proof the Warrens' car was in Lake Crescent. With many clues discovered thus far, the only really positive proof could be for some lucky person to somehow hook the Warren car with a grapple and raise it to the surface. It was hoped that whoever might try to recover it would perhaps use the Port Angeles Western Railroad magnet that was used to locate the steam shovel in Lake Crescent several years earlier.

While visiting Madrona Point on Monday, September 2, William Vert of Joyce, a small town near Crescent Bay, north of Lake Crescent, discovered a light-colored cap in the water just west of the crash site and near the shore. The man's cap was obscured by overhanging brush and had apparently been washed into the concealed spot by wave action. Sheriff Pike and his investigators had missed the cap when the area was first searched. Mr. Vert brought the cap to the Sheriff's office in Port Angeles and told Sheriff Pike the circumstances behind the discovery. Pike showed the cap to the two Warren boys in hopes of identifying the cap as property of their missing parents. Frank Warren, immediately identified the cap as belonging to his father. He stated, *"Sure, that's Dad's."* Charles, could not positively identify the cap as belonging to his father.

Up to this point, all evidence pointed toward the Warrens and their car being in Lake Crescent.

Evidence found by Sheriff Pike's team:

• Sun visor from a Chevrolet car of the same model as the Warrens.

• A distinctive flower vase identified as either the vase, or one just like it, that was placed in the car by the former owner.

• A cap positively identified by Frank Warren as belonging to his father.

• Wheel marks near the water indicating a vehicle had left the roadway.

• Limbs torn from a cedar tree near and in the water indicating the path of the car as it slid down the slope into the lake.

• Broken glass on the lake bottom possibly from the windshield.

Sheriff Pike concluded his investigation, and the case were suspended pending any new evidence. New evidence wouldn't appear for another 73 years.

On Tuesday, September 17, Sidney Alton, Russell Warren's uncle, arrived in Port Angeles from North Dakota to meet with local authorities to learn more about the disappearance of his nephew. He had left his home in early September traveling to Port Angeles. While en route and traveling through Spokane, he was recruited to fight forest fires near Yakima. He was therefore delayed by several weeks in arriving in Port Angeles. He would have likely met Blanche's mother had he arrived as originally planned. Apparently, Blanche's side of the family did not communicate well with Russell's side of the family. Sheriff Pike took Mr. Alton to Lake Crescent and showed him the very spot where the car disappeared into the water.

Additionally, Robert A. Warren, Russell's oldest brother, wrote a letter to the Port Angeles Evening News on September 23, 1929 asking for information about his missing brother. He had not been informed of the disappearance and wanted to know what happened to his two nephews. His address in Milwaukee, Wisconsin, was 682 Reed Street. Robert apparently was not close to his brother and had not seen Russell since he moved to Washington State seven years earlier.

The two boys left Port Angeles with Blanche's mother after it became apparent that Sheriff Pike had exhausted all of his options to find, "*The Missing Ones*", as Bertha said in her letter. The three left Port Angeles sometime during the second week of September and just missed seeing Sidney Alton, Russell's uncle who arrived in Port Angeles on September 17.

This is a photo taken about 1907 of the Rhone family. Bertha Alton Rhone is at the far left with Blanche at the far right. The young boy is Blanche's brother, William. Blanche's grandmother, Mary Louise Alton is pictured. Courtesy of the Warren family.

On September 29, 1929, the U.S. Stock Market crashed and millions of Americans were to see their lives drastically change forever. Jobs were lost, savings disappeared, and farms were foreclosed upon when loans could not be paid. For the next 10 years, a Great Depression enveloped Americans as they struggled to feed their families and find a job. The Warren family was no exception.

7

THE TWO BOYS

Charles and Frank had been in the care of their Grandmother Bertha since late August. Around September 17th, with winter fast approaching, Bertha brought the boys back to her farm in Heron Montana. Heron is a small town in far northwestern Montana near the Idaho border. It is not far from Sandpoint, Idaho and Spokane Washington, near the Clark Fork River and near train service. Heron is surrounded by high Rocky Mountain peaks and numerous lakes. It would seem that this would be a perfect place for two young boys to settle into a new life with seemingly unlimited hunting and fishing just out the back door. Bertha's husband, Venning Matteson, fixed up the chicken coop as best he could to accommodate the boys, who would live there during the cold Montana winter.

Bertha's first husband and Blanche's natural father was John Francis (Frank) Rhone. Blanche's mother, Bertha, married John Rhone in 1894 in Wisconsin and together produced six children. Two of the children lived to adulthood, Blanche was one of them. John Francis Rhone mysteriously disappeared in Iowa in July of 1905. His disappearance is just another strange event in the whole Warren-Rhone family lore. Bertha later married a Venning Matteson at Sand Point, Idaho, in 1927. The boys would know Venning as their step-grandfather.

Soon after the two boys arrived at the Matteson farm, 14 year old Frank decided living in a chicken coop was not for him. He left the farm to live in Clark Fork, Idaho about 15 miles away with other relatives. According to Louise Alton Allen (Swiggum) who was about the same age and a cousin of the boys (I was lucky enough to interview her), Frank was not fond of his grandmother and considered her to be a very difficult woman, referring to her as *"an old battle axe."*

Young Charles, perhaps taken at the Matteson farm in Heron, Montana. His new family taught him to trap and skin animals, selling the skins to make extra money. Courtesy of the Warren family.

As the Great Depression tightened its grip on America, families did whatever it took to hang on to their homes, land and farms. Bertha took a job at a hotel in Spokane, in late October to help earn some extra income. Bill Rhone (Blanche's brother) and his wife, Irene, also lived in Heron, near the Matteson farm. Bill and his wife would get to know the boys and help care for them, especially Charles, who would occasionally live with them until he finished school. It was a good thing to have family members around during tough economic times. Charles learned how to trap fur animals from Bill Rhone, and sold the fur.

At age 19, Charles moved to Clark Fork It is uncertain if he moved to be with his older brother who already lived there. Clark Fork was a mere 15 miles downstream from Heron. A short time later, Charles moved to Aberdeen, Washington (southeast of Forks, Washington and about one hundred miles south of Lake Crescent). Perhaps there was a desire to move back to the Olympic Peninsula to be close to the place where his parents disappeared, although there is no evidence to suggest that was the case. He found work nearby in the lucrative logging industry and perhaps learned commercial fishing.

The 1940 wedding photo of Charles and Mildred Warren in Aberdeen, Washington. Courtesy of the Warren family.

At age 23, Charles married Mildred Granger of Hoquiam, Washington (Aberdeen and Hoquiam are neighboring cities), on May 4, 1940. Together they raised three children, Roland (Rollie), Patricia (Patti), and Phoebe. In 1945, the family moved to Wallipa, Washington and moved again in 1954 to McKinleyville, California near the northern coast. Roland married and moved back to Washington State. Patricia married and moved to Oklahoma. Phoebe married and stayed in California. Charles continued to work in the logging industry until 1954. He took up commercial fishing and bought a 35 foot salmon fishing boat renaming it the Mildred G.

On June 14, 1964, Charles and his fishing boat failed to return to port after a trip to the open ocean. An extensive search for he and his fishing boat revealed only debris floating on the surface of the ocean. An investigation revealed that a Japanese ship had been in the same area and probably rammed his tiny fishing boat, sending it and Charles to the bottom of the sea. Charles's remains were never recovered, and a death certificate was never issued, just like his parents 35 years before. Mildred remarried in 1968.

Frank's life was somewhat different. Shortly after arriving at the Matteson Farm in Montana, he decided that chicken coop life was not for him. As mentioned before, his relationship with his grandmother was apparently not good. In mid-October of 1929, at age 14 ½, Frank left the farm in Heron and may have moved to Clark Fork Idaho to live with relatives. A year later, he reportedly lied about his age and joined the Merchant Marines. However, his son Dennis stated that his father was never in the Merchant Marines and is not sure where the story came from. A few years later, Frank married a woman from Clark Fork and had one child named Peter. He divorced her and married Edith Ann Hanson on March 11, 1939. Over the coming years, the couple had four children, Kay, who died at eight months; Dennis, who died in November of 2000; and Sandra and James. Sandra later married and stayed in Idaho. James lives in California.

When the United States entered World War II, Frank joined the Navy and fought in the Pacific against the Japanese. Frank always had a great love for water just as Charles did. After the war, Frank returned to Clark Fork. He later moved back to Western Washington, perhaps to be close to where his parents had disappeared or perhaps to obtain work. Maybe it was just a place he was familiar with, having been raised in the area as a child.

Although there is nothing to suggest that either of the two brothers ever visited Lake Crescent after 1929 to visit the site their parents disappeared, they were living on the Olympic Peninsula and not too far from the site their parents disappeared. At some point, they must have driven toward Port Angeles on the Olympic Highway. They likely drove by Madrona Point or Ambulance Point or Meldrim Point, whatever name was used at the time. If either of them did, it would be easy to picture Frank or Charles or perhaps both brothers together, standing along the south shore of the Lake at a little beach just west of Madrona Point, looking out over the water wondering what the truth really was. They likely read the local newspapers, reading every now and then about a boat or motor vehicle accidents at Lake Crescent. The lake was now part of Olympic National Park. Perhaps, they wondered, someone, maybe the Park Rangers or a local dive club, sport divers, or fisherman would accidently stumble upon a rusted old car at the bottom of the Lake containing the bodies of two people.

Scuba diving was a new sport in the late 1950s and early 1960s. Perhaps a sport diver would take up the search in a way that hard hat divers in 1929 could not. Did the boys still hold a slight hope that someday someone would knock at their door and tell them their parents had been found? Charles Warren's only son, Roland, stated that his father never talked much about his loss because it brought up a time in his life of great sadness, frustration and irreconcilable mental anguish.

Frank died of pulmonary congestion and edema at age 57 in Palmer, Washington, on August 12, 1972.

The sad truth is that Frank and Charles both died before they should have like their parents many years ago. They lived their entire lives never knowing what really happened to their parents.

Left to right, is Bill, Irene and Ed Sayer, Mildred Granger (wife of Charles) Charles and Frank Warren. Photo was taken sometime around 1941 or 1942 probably in Aberdeen Washington, by Louise Allen and is provided courtesy of the Warren family.

8

DIVER BOB CASO

Robert G. Caso was born in New Jersey n 1924. He lived in Union City and graduated from Union Hill High School in 1943. Bob joined the Navy as a fireman in 1943 during World War II and was stationed in Port Angeles aboard the *USS Eagle 57*, a 200 foot patrol boat similar to a Coast Guard cutter.

Bob married Louise Kiser, a native of Port Angeles in November of 1945. He left the Navy and Port Angeles one year later and moved back to New Jersey with his wife. In 1948, Bob and his wife returned to Port Angeles with Bob having found work in the local harbor he knew so well, as a longshoreman. He spent the next 43 years working in that capacity. They had three children, Michael, Robin, and Darcie. Robin was killed in a car accident on May 12, 1973, by a drunk driver.

Bob has a wiry build, an active mind and a quick laugh. As a young boy, he nearly drowned on the Jersey Shore but was saved by his uncle from the waters of the Atlantic. After that, his father taught him to swim and he quickly came to love the water. Bob's Navy career strengthened his interest in water recreation.

In 1952, a company called Aqua Lung™ began marketing the sport of scuba-diving to the general public in the United States. Aqua Lung™, a company started by Frenchmen Jacque Cousteau and Emile Gagnon, developed the self-contained underwater breathing apparatus (scuba) during World War II as a tool to assist the French Navy with a range of underwater military applications. The device they invented was a rendition of a medical oxygen-demand valve used in hospitals. Cousteau and Gagnon simply modified the device by installing a stronger valve spring and diaphragm and added a special hose and mouthpiece. The U.S. Navy used scuba toward the end of the war, and Bob witnessed what the new equipment was capable of.

In 1953, Bob decided to take up the rather new sport of scuba diving. Bob and his friends realized that scuba could take them to underwater sights that no one had ever seen. The dream of being totally free of cables and ropes, surface-support air hoses, heavy weights, and lead shoes was within reach. Imagine being able to swim like a fish for extended periods of time with the ability to venture into deep water. Some of Bob's Navy friends were trained as military divers, and with Bob's strong interest and ability in water, it was a natural progression.

Diving in the 1950s was only for the most adventurous spirits. Prior to World War II, extended dives used surface supplied air, brass helmets and heavy lead boots, much like the 1920s and 1930s. A diver could only walk on the bottom of a lake or ocean. Swimming was not possible. But that was all about to change for many water sport enthusiasts, including a bunch of local adventurers in a small town in far western Washington State.

In 1953, Bob and two of his friends purchased three complete sets of dive gear that included a Bel Aqua dry suit, mask, fins, gloves, single steel compressed air cylinder and Aqua Lung™ double hose regulator. The three friends manufactured their own lead weight belts.

While doing research on the new sport of scuba diving, Caso visited the local library in Port Angeles. He asked the librarian for books and magazines on shipwrecks. Bob was especially interested in shipwrecks like Spanish Galleons where he could find a cannon or some treasure. He was keenly interested in stories about shipwrecks such as the *Diamond Knot*, which sank in 1946 off Crescent Beach with seven million cans of Atlantic salmon aboard. Seeing a ship loaded with treasure was every adventurer's dream. Bob and his friends were on the cutting edge of a new sport that had the potential for great adventure. They later formed a local dive club called NEMGORF, or frogmen spelled backward. The club was off to a good start.

The librarian gave Bob a stack of magazines, folders, and newspaper articles. Amongst the newspaper articles were old news clippings telling the story of the disappearance of Blanche and Russell Warren. Bob read the articles with great interest and knew that his new scuba gear would be the right tool to finally put closure to the Warren case. Bob returned to the library many times over the next year analyzing the geology of the lake, taking notes from old newspaper articles and researching old police reports. He put together a three-ring binder that stayed with him for many years, a binder that he eventually gave to me.

In 1954, Charles and Frank Warren would have been 37 and 39 years old and very much alive. They were both married with children. Charles was living a mere 210 miles away in Wallipa Bay, Washington, south of the Olympic Peninsula. If Charles or Frank had known that local divers with new scuba technology were about to search Lake Crescent a second time, I'm sure they would have been frequent visitors to Port Angeles. Because they loved the water, perhaps they would have even taken up the sport of diving to assist with the search effort. According to Bob Caso, he never knew that the two Warren boys were still alive and living in Washington. If Bob had known they lived in the State, he said he would have contacted them.

Blanche's mother, Bertha Matteson was also still alive and living in California. I'm sure she would have been very interested in knowing local divers with new scuba technology were dive into mysterious Lake Crescent, the lake that had presumably taken the lives of her daughter and son-in-law 26 years earlier.

Bob's first dry suit was a Bel Aqua two-piece suit. He had to wear thick, long underwear and wool socks to stay warm. The theory was to keep dry unlike a west suit which was still a few years away. The suit was made of rubber and had no inflator valve or pressure-relief valve. Air was added to the suit by blowing air into the neck seal, a technique that was difficult at best to manage underwater! The air in the suit was released by opening up the neck seal while underwater. The diver usually got wet and cold. Divers had to be very careful when descending and ascending, as suit squeeze was a common problem. Suit squeeze was very painful and occurred when water pressure compressed the air in the suit, decreasing the ability of the suit to provide thermal protection. Air needed to be added to the inside of the suit to provide buoyancy, otherwise the diver would become heavier as the diver continued to descend into deeper water. Air also needed to be added to the suit to provide insulation necessary to ward off cold water temperatures. Bob also used an Aqua Lung™ double hose regulator, a steel compressed-air cylinder, and a lead weight belt to compensate for the buoyancy of the dry suit. There was no buoyancy compensator vest to adjust for depth in those days. Bob also had a Cornelius air compressor needed to fill the dive club scuba cylinders. The compressor could pump out two cubic feet of air per minute, up to 3000 PSI.

Bob and the NEMGORF club worked on the Warren case as time permitted. The club divers searched for the Warren car in the area of Ambulance (Meldrim) Point during the summer months of 1956 and 1957. According to Bob Caso, they never did identify the exact location, near the *"little curve in the highway"* where sheriff Pike had recovered evidence in 1929. By coincidence, Bob and his dive buddies probably dove at the exact spot where Sheriff Pike and his investigative team found the lower vase, sun visor, windshield glass. However, they did not find evidence related to the Warren case. They searched the water to depths of about ninety feet east, north, and west of Ambulance Point, as it was called then. According to Bob Caso, they were looking for the 1927 Chevy sedan the Warrens were driving and were not looking for small, subtle clues. After two years of initial searching at various locations around the lake, they did not find any clues that would have led them to believe they were in the right area.

Left to right, Bob Caso, Chuck Widden and Dick Owen. These men were members of the NEMGORF dive club. The photo was taken at Rocky Point along the shores of Lake Crescent on May 14, 1955. Note the dry suits and double hose regulators. Courtesy of Bob Caso.

Bob and the NEMGORF Club worked on the Warren case as time permitted. They searched for the Warren car in the area of Ambulance (Meldrim) Point during the summer months of 1956 and 1957. According to Caso, they never did identify the exact location reportedly near the "*little curve in the highway*" where sheriff Pike had recovered evidence in 1929. By coincidence, Bob and his dive buddies probably dove the exact spot where Sheriff Pike and his investigative team found the flower vase, sun visor and windshield glass. The NEMGORF divers did not report finding any evidence related to the Warren case. They searched the water to depths of about 90 feet east, north, and west of Ambulance Point, as it was called then. According to Bob Caso, they were looking for the 1927 Chevy sedan the Warrens were driving and not really looking for small, subtle clues. After two years of searching at various locations around the lake, they found nothing that would have led them to believe they were in the right area.

Remarkably, the clues were there then just as they were when we looked in 2001. But they were subtle. Perhaps it just wasn't time for Lake Crescent to give up her secrets.

Another diver in the Port Angeles area was Johnny Sweatt, a local Port Angeles police officer and later a deputy with the Clallam County Sheriff's Department and a founding member of the NEMGORF dive club. Sweatt developed an underwater sled that divers could ride while being towed by a boat. The divers could adjust the depth of the sled by moving the wings up or down. The sled made it much easier to search the bottom of the lake. The sled was indeed used at Lake Crescent in the area of Meldrim Point. However, the divers needed to dive below 90 feet, something those riding the dive sled did not want to do.

Bob Caso also remembered the dangers of diving at Meldrim Point with its extremely steep drop offs. He recalled talking with the other NEMGROF divers about Meldrim Point and how if they did not use extreme caution diving in the area, they would die. Bob was very concerned about the depth of the water and the steep underwater terrain.

In 1956, Bob visited Jack Pike, the newly retired police officer, sheriff and game officer, at his home in Port Angeles. Pike told him many stories about hunting, fishing, and moonshine cases he had investigated over his long law enforcement career. One he fondly remembered was a moonshine case in which he hid in the tall grass along a small canyon, waiting for the moonshine makers to come out of the woods. He didn't find the suspects but later found out from the moonshine runners that while in his hiding place, he was lying on a pipe that was part of the still operation. The two talked about many things in Jack's career, but they never talked about the Warren case. Interestingly, that was Bob Caso's purpose in talking to Pike in the first place. A few years later, Jack Pike moved to Reedsport, Oregon, to live with his daughter, Lillian, who would care for him. Bob never saw Jack Pike again.

Not all of Bob Caso's efforts in the Warren investigation were water related. About 1955, Bob said he talked by telephone to the nurse who took care of Blanche Warren while she was at the Lincoln Hospital. The nurse told him that Russell carried out two pieces of luggage when he left with Blanche on that fateful day of July 3, 1929. That would suggest that Blanche may have been in the hospital for more than just a few days. Bob asked the nurse why Blanche was in the hospital, but the nurse could not remember what her medical issue was. Bob could not recall the name of the nurse. The nurse had long since retired but did remember the Warren case, clearly hoping that searchers would find the missing couple.

Bob knew what it was like to lose a loved one. His young 21 year old daughter, Robin, was killed by a drunk driver outside of Port Angeles in 1973. Understandably, he took her death very hard. When I visited him in his home for the first time in 2001, a large photograph of his beautiful daughter was set up on a painter's easel in the living room in a prominent place. She was smiling brightly, perhaps enjoying a summer day in her youth. She looked happy, young, and full of life. Those were probably Bob's last memories of her.. He felt the terrible loneliness and vacancy when someone you love so dearly leaves without ever saying goodbye. Years later, Bob would again remember the two boys who had been left behind when their mother and father disappeared without an explanation. Bob never forgot and never gave up.

On April 13, 2001, Bob came to the Storm King Ranger Station and told me the story of the missing Warren's, Blanche and Russell.

9

THE RANGERS

I thought about the case for about two weeks before I decided to take what information I had to Chief Ranger Curt Sauer and to Barb Maynes, the park's Public Information Officer. I needed to get Curt's approval to work on the case. Barb needed to be well informed because of the unusual nature of the case and the potential for a lot of media interest. I knew that a case like this was probably a low priority because of funding and personnel shortages. It seemed like we never had enough money or people to get the job done to our own high standards. What would tax payers think of spending tax money on an old case that we had a slim possibility of solving? Because of this, I was willing to give the mystery a considerable amount of my own time.

I had the park's dispatch office issue a case incident number for the investigation, which would allow us to track and document the incident for historical purposes. I wrote a short case-incident report with the known facts and went to Port Angeles to meet with the Chief Ranger. In his office, I briefed him on what I knew about the case and what I thought we could do about it. I explained to him the public-relations benefits to the park and our desire to use the case to get to know the submerged resources of Lake Crescent. I really felt strongly that this could be a very good public-relations event. Many of the people living in the area were very knowledgeable about local history. This would be a great opportunity to connect with the community. In addition, we could use the case as an opportunity to train the dive team on search tactics and deep water diving certification maintenance.

The Warren case fit rather well with the park goals to discover new information about the cultural resources in Olympic National Park.. Not much was known about the submerged lands of Olympic National Park, and this was a golden opportunity to get to know the resources we were charged with protecting. At the time, there was an initiative throughout the National Park Service system to inventory and monitor sensitive and threatened natural and cultural resources

We knew that submerged trees standing perfectly upright in deep water or lying down in some cases, suggested that Lake Crescent had a much different level thousands of years ago. We later discovered the Lake level changed about 5,990 years ago as a result of a landslide on the east end of the lake and that the area had seen significant landslide activity. Native people told legends of s lides, which likely contributed to various lake levels. The native population of fish in Lake Crescent, long isolated from their parent stock, added to the mystery of how the area's geology, fish and wildlife, and native people lived and evolved together.

The Chief Ranger, after consulting with the Assistant Superintendent, Roger Rudolph, gave his permission to use the case as a training opportunity. The f irst order of business was to try to f ind the accident location Sheriff Pike had talked about and described. I reread the 1929 newspaper articles and found the site where Sheriff Pike recovered evidence was named Madrona Point. A quick check of the US Geological Survey topographic map of Lake Crescent did not show a place around the shorelines named Madrona Point. Many of the other points of land were prominently named and were well known.

Another map named a point of land that jutted north from the south shore with a name not commonly used by locals and Rangers, and that was Meldrim Point. However, the newspapers stated that the elusive Madrona Point was about one mile east of Fairholm, a well-known landmark at the far west end of Lake Crescent. A point of land that jutted out from the south shore, one mile east of Fairholm, along the old Olympic Highway was unfamiliar named, Meldrim Point. But everyone, including the Rangers, now called it Ambulance Point.

In early May while on patrol, I stopped at there and examined the shore line, road, and turnout. It certainly did not look like the place Sheriff Pike described many years ago. I had trouble visualizing this as the place described by Pike. First, Ambulance Point is not exactly a *"little curve in the highway."* It is a rather sharp and long curve. Secondly, it has a shoreline that does not drop off abruptly near the roadway, as was described in 1929. Thirdly, a car driving west along the Olympic Highway approaching this spot and then leaving the roadway would come to rest in relatively shallow water near the roadway, unless the road and the shoreline had changed due to construction. The deepest water in which a car could come to rest appeared to be 50 to 60 feet east or west of here. I telephoned seasonal Ranger John Ward living in California. He was one of the first divers on the park dive team in the late 1960s and a 35 year veteran of seasonal employment at Olympic National Park. John had not arrived in the park yet and would not return until early June. He was a veteran of many body-recoveries and property-salvage operations at Lake Crescent. If any diver would know about old cars and objects in the lake, John or fellow seasonal Ranger diver Art Sandison would be the guys who would know. John had not heard of Madrona Point nor had he heard the Warren story before.

I telephoned Art Sandison who lived in southern Washington State. He had been working at Olympic National Park for 35 years as a seasonal Park Ranger. Art was also one of the early divers on the park dive team and like John, had spent a lot of time underwater at Lake Crescent. He had also never heard of the Warren mystery and did not have a recollection of a place called Madrona Point.

I contacted Ranger Larry Lang, another long-time Lake Crescent Ranger and former Dive Officer for the park. He was still working for the park but was now assigned to work out of the headquarters area in Port Angeles. Larry had also not heard of the Warren mystery and did not know where Madrona Point was.

It appeared as though the Warren disappearance was completely unknown to the park employees and the citizens in the local area. After 72 years the Warren case had been forgotten. It was time to bring the cold Warren case back to life and hopefully find the answers that the two Warren boys had been surely seeking their entire lives.

We needed to begin the search for the Warrens in a special way.. I had a feeling that is was going to be an extraordinary experience and what better way to start the search than to start than at the highest probability area with a dive operation, an area we knew nothing about, Ambulance Point.

We brought the dive team together and discussed the options, all agreeing an exploratory dive at Ambulance Point slated for Tuesday, July 3, 2001, 72 years to the day the Warrens disappeared, was our best option, given the minimal and nebulous information we had. Maybe we would get lucky.

Ranger divers Tony Lutz, Lynn Roberson, Art Sandison, John Ward and Dan Messaros all converged at Ambulance Point at 12:30 p.m. on that Tuesday, to dive the site. Our mission was to search the area for potential clues and to determine what the underwater topography was like east and west of the point. The water temperature was a cool 55 degrees with 70 to 80 feet of visibility. The diving conditions were excellent. The air temperature was in the mid 60's, sunny with thin high clouds and a moderate northwest wind. The weather was exactly the same as it was 72 years before.

I was supposed to dive, but I was on light duty. I separated my left shoulder one week before playing softball in the local Port Angeles league. However, I was not going to miss all the fun.. Led by the newly appointed Park Dive Officer, Ranger Dan Messaros, the four other divers searched the water close to shore looking for clues. The water was about 20 to 40 feet deep. I had never been diving at this particular site because there didn't appear to be any attractions. It wasn't a popular site for other divers either. Our team used the beach area on the east side of the point to stage the dive. The Kingfisher Ranger patrol boat was beached nearby in the event a diver had trouble. Each diver was equipped with styrofoam float called Pelican Buoy used to mark artifacts in the event something significant was found. The dive lasted about 35 minutes.

Returning to the surface, each diver gave a report of what they had seen. Lutz reported that he saw many old car parts and a lot of trash, but nothing that looked like the wreck of an old car. He noted rather consistent depths on the north, west, and east sides of the point and did not see an area that dropped off "*to an unknown depth near the roadway*" as Sheriff Pike described 72 years before. Lynn Roberson reported seeing a rusty, vehicle bumper but was not able to determine how old it was. That was something we would check out later. The other divers didn't see any obvious clues but did say the underwater terrain didn't match what we were looking for. I was not convinced Ambulance Point was the right spot and was not sure we should continue to look here.

A few days later, I talked to Bob Caso about the dives we had done at Ambulance Point and the topography there. He told me about the dives his club had done at the site over 40 years ago, including the use of the dive sled. He gave me a series of bathometric maps of Lake Crescent produced in the 1970s by Peninsula College Fisheries Department. Bob explain the gradients near the edge of the road as they appeared in the bathometric map. They unfortunately were not in fine enough detail to identify sheer underwater cliffs near the roadway. What we were looking for was a place where the lake bottom dropped away from the shore line very quickly. This drop off had to be near the "*little curve in the highway.*"

When I returned to work the next day, it occurred to me that two years earlier two seasonal Park Fishery Technicians had conducted a fresh-water mussel survey of the lake. They had conducted a snorkel survey of the shallow waters near shore around the entire Lake. I called John Southard, one of the technicians, and asked him if he had ever seen an area in the lake near shore that dropped off abruptly and was also close to the road. Somewhere in the back of my mind, I thought I remembered him telling me about an old car in the lake. I explained to him the reason for my search, that we were looking for one that may still contain two people who disappeared 72 years ago. John, in a rather calm voice, said, *"I know where there is an old car near the edge of the roadway, and it's in about fifty feet of water. The car is located east of Barnes Point near the Rock Screen. You can find it from the lake by diving near the old concrete crib work that supports the roadway."*

When he finished, I was rather excited about the prospect of diving the site, hoping it was the missing car. John went on to describe the car as an old sedan, very rusty, sitting on the bottom near Milepost 229 of Highway 101. Milepost 229 is 7 miles east of the west end of the lake and certainly not near the area Sheriff Pike talked about 72 years ago. Nonetheless, this was reported as an old car seen on the bottom of the lake near the edge of the road and in deep water. It was also in an area seldom visited by divers. Could this be the missing Warren car or another car?

I wasted no time telephoning Dan Messaros. telling him John's story . We discussed diving the site once my shoulder healed a bit more, perhaps around the beginning of August.

A few days later, I called another former Dive Officer and a long-time Ranger at Lake Crescent, Mike Butler. Mike had worked at the Lake well over 10 years and knew the lake as well as anyone except perhaps John Ward. Mike knew a great deal about the underwater attractions of the lake. I told him the story of my meeting with Bob Caso and about the Warren's. I asked him if he had ever heard of the them before, and he like everyone else, had not. He told me the Warren story was probably just another lake story embellished by time. I asked Mike if he had ever heard of Madrona Point, and he had not. I gave him the description the newspaper had of the Madrona Point. Mike told me the description sounded like Sledgehammer Point, a curve in the road where accidents were frequent. Mike said that a log truck and car could just barely squeeze by each other at Sledgehammer Point without swapping paint. That was before the 1986 road work that straightened and widened Sledgehammer Point..

During the second week of July, I telephoned Tom Tinkham and asked him all the same questions. Tom was a local resident who lived on Lake Crescent in a lakeshore house directly north and within sight of Ambulance Point. He was born and raised on Lake Crescent and had very good memories of the Lake from the 1940s including an extensive photo collection. Tom had never heard of Madrona Point or of the Warren mystery either. He did tell me he thought Madrona Point could be Sledgehammer Point because that point had a lot of Madrona trees on it.

Ed Brooks, 45 years old, was the grandson of Ed Brooks, and grandnephew of Harry Brooks, both pioneers on the lake. It was the elder Ed and Harry who both assisted with the search for the Warrens. The younger Ed was a maintenance worker for the park and, of all places, at Lake Crescent. Ed knew everyone in the area and said he would ask local people if they knew of Madrona Point. He would also ask his elderly father. A few days later Ed told me that his father had no recollection of the Warren disappearance or of the elusive Madrona Point. Finding it was getting frustration and more work than I thought it would be.. There must be at least one local resident who knew where Madrona Point was.

So far, all my investigative efforts had drawn a blank. On Thursday, August 2, Dan Messaros, Lynn Roberson, and I finally decided to dive and search for the old car described by the Fishery Technician John Southard. This could be the car we were looking for, even though the location was 1.5 miles east of Barnes Point rather than 1.5 miles east of Fairholm. Perhaps a mistake had been made in the newspaper article, or maybe Sheriff Pike was mistaken about the Madrona Point site. Pike knew the area around the lake very well so it was not likely that he would make such a mistake. But it was something we still needed to check out. To get to this dive site, we utilized the park dive boat equipped with a dive ladder and platform. The boat was also equipped with a Global Positioning System (GPS). On the day of the dive the skies were partly cloudy and the lake temperature was a cool but very clear 66 degrees. Documenting what we hoped would be the missing Warren car was going to be important. We brought the park owned Nikonos V 35-mm underwater film camera and the Sony VX 1000 digital video camera housed in a Ikelite waterproof case .

1931 Ford Model A sedan near Milepost 229. There is a large section of guardrail in the passenger side seat. The engine is missing as well as all the tires, transmission and read end. The vehicle had been stripped of all valuable parts. Courtesy of Olympic National Park.

I had never been diving here before. We hit the water and swam on the surface away from shore, then slowly dropped to 50 feet, the depth suggested by John Southard. Visibility was about 50 to 60 feet with plenty of visible light from the surface. Dive conditions were excellent. I saw that the lake bottom dropped away from the edge of the road very quickly. It was also easy to see that at one time the old road bed was three or four feet lower.

As we descended, we could see a lot of sharp, angular rocks typical of ones that had been blasted from the cliff face on the side of the road and had likely been pushed into the water during the 1986 project that elevated the road. We found the frame of a badly rusted old car in 45 feet of water in the exact location John Southard had described. It had no doors, roof, engine, wheels, tires, axles, or transmission. The radiator was missing. In fact most of the car was gone. The parts that could have produced an easy identification were rusted away or missing. The interior of the car was entirely missing. All the glass was missing from the windows and there was no evidence of human remains. The car looked like it had been stripped. We photographed the site. It did appeared to be about the right age and style of 1927 Chevy sedan that the Warrens were driving. But the location of this wreck was not anywhere near the west end of Lake Crescent.

A few days after the dive, I had to conduct some business at one of the local dive shops in Port Angeles, Port Angeles Sound Dive. John Southard was now working at the store as the manager and no longer worked for the park. When I arrived at the shop, John was not working, but one of his employees was, Dathan Meyers, also a diver. I told him the story about the disappearance of the Warren's and about Bob Caso and the NEMGORF dive club. I also told him about our search for the 1927 Chevy sedan.

I described the condition of the car we had found near the Rock Screen and told him that I wanted to know what happened to this car so that I could identify it. I mentioned the engine would have features that would help identify the manufacturer of the car. Dathan then told me he knew of a diver that owned a dive store named Bubbles Below in Woodinville, Washington. . He had heard a story about a diver that had removed a car engine out of Lake Crescent and had it in the dive shop as a show piece.

I knew that over the years, many divers had removed artifacts, some of cultural value to the park, like old railroad gear, resort artifacts such as old bottles and dishes, and some recent lost-and-found property from swimmers and boats such as sunglasses and jewelry. A lot of these divers falsely believed that if they didn't take it, someone else would. Many divers simply did not understand or know the laws prohibiting artifact hunting. The clerk told me the owner of the shop was Bud Gray. I had never been to a dive shop called Bubbles Below, and I had never met Bud Gray, but I was hoping to soon.

That weekend, I drove up to Woodinville to find the dive shop and Bud. I found it in a small strip mall tucked into a corner. The shop looked clean, well- kept and the inventory looked healthy. As I walked into the shop, a rather attractive female clerk was behind the counter and asked if I needed help. I explained that I was just looking around but that I wanted to meet the store owner. I also saw a man behind the counter who exhibited a commanding presence and whom I guessed was Bud Gray, the owner. He was just finishing up with a customer, so I decided to wait, hoping that I could talk to him.

A few minutes later, the customer left the store, and I approached Bud. I explained that I was led to believe an old automobile engine was on display in here that had come from Lake Crescent. Bud told me there was no engine on display in his store. I went on the say him I was a National Park Ranger from Olympic National Park and that I that I didn't want the engine back. I just wanted to look at the model and make in hopes of identifying the car we recently found at Lake Crescent.

I went on to tell Gray about the Warrens. I could tell Bud liked a good dive story and it appeared to me he liked the story I had just told him. He knew of a couple of guys who might be able to help, one in particular who had done many dives in Lake Crescent and might know about cars in the lake. Ones of these guys may even know the locations of the Warren car. He told me to contact Bill Walker and another man who did photography work, John Rawlings. He gave me both of their phone numbers.

As I walked out the door of the dive shop, it occurred to me that the conversation I had just had would probably be very fruitful. Even though the story about an old car engine being in his shop was likely just embellishment, it did turn out to be a useful clue. You never know when a false lead will turn into something dynamic. The name Bill Walker, for some reason, sounded familiar. I had never heard of John Rawlings before, but I was soon to get to know him very well.

A few days later, Dan Messaros, Art Sandison and I returned to the car site with our dive gear and splashed into the 65 degree water. We took a lot of underwater video with our new digital video camera in an effort to figure out all the features. The three of us searched the site and captured about ten minutes of video. We finished the dive knowing the two dives had completed our objective of finding and documenting the car John Southard had told us about. When we returned to the dive locker, we hooked up the video camera to the television set. The video would allow us to examine the evidence at the site in much greater detail and for as long as we wished. There were lots of large rocks that had struck the vehicle and had partially buried it. There was a section of guard rail that impaled the auto, and it was bent in nearly a complete circle.

My first thought when seeing the pictures of the guardrail was that it was part of a washing machine, but it was clearly a section of guardrail. Thank goodness for the video camera. We reported our findings to Chief Ranger Curt Sauer and briefed the Park's Public Information Officer, Barbara Maynes. Barbara was very interested in the story. I explained to her I believed this could be a very good community-relations story. She agreed to write a press release and send it out to the local and regional newspapers, hoping that the story would generate some interest and possibly lead to a clue or a person who knew about the Warren story. I was hoping to have success with the media much like Sheriff Pike had done 72 years earlier.

A few days later, the *Peninsula Daily News* ran the press release written by Barb Maynes. The story made the *Associated Press* and was picked up by many of the regional newspapers including the *Aberdeen World*, the *Seattle Post-Intelligencer*, and the Olympia, Washington newspapers. Maybe an elderly person in the community would read the story and come forward with a statement that they witnessed some of the events and search efforts of 1929.

Toward the middle of August 2001, I called the Chevy dealer in Port Angeles and asked if they knew of any 1927 automobiles in Port Angeles. I was to contact a man living in Port Angeles named Robert Frick, who, at one time had owned a local welding and metal-fabrication shop. He owned an old Chevy sedan. I phoned him and gave him the brief version of the Warren story, one he already knew after reading the newspaper. He did own a 1927 Chevy sedan that was in parts in his garage and was restoring it. He said I could come by and take a look at it. I was very interested in taking photographs and measurements of the doors and windows as these would be unique to this brand of auto. This was my first look at the brand and model of car the Warrens had driven.

I expected to see an auto nearly built but was slightly disappointed to see that it was completely disassembled. My disappointment was short lived though, because it turned out that I was able to see the car in much greater detail and take very accurate measurements of the doors and windows. The visit with Mr. Frick convinced me beyond a doubt the car we had seen at the Rock Screen near Milepost 229 was not a Chevrolet and was not the Warren car. Mr. Frick's 1927 Chevrolet was much different in dimensions and style than one we had recently dove one. The doors and windows were all of different dimensions. Mr. Frick said 1927 Chevy automobiles had many unique features that separated them from other cars of their day. One feature was that a significant amount of the car was made of wood, including some of the frame. Another feature was the design of running lights known as milk lights mounted on the hood forward of the windshield. The small, milk-colored-lights and the style were unique to Chevy automobiles. Ford did have similar lights, but mounted them on a bracket or brace.

A few days later, I took the still pictures and video of the car we found at Milepost 229 to Ranger John Ward and Dr. Paul Gleeson, the Chief of Cultural Resources. Dr. Gleeson recommended that I show them to Dr. Fred York, the Service's Pacific West Support Office Archaeologist, who had some notoriety for his expertise with old cars. I emailed the pictures to Dr. York. Early during the next week, he called to tell me that the pictures were of a Ford Model A. Dr. York stated the gas cap just aft of the engine bay up on the hood near the windshield, was a dead giveaway. All Ford Model A's had the gas cap in that location. The gas cap on a 1927 Chevrolet was at the back of the car where the gas tank was located. Dr. York also said the car in Lake Crescent looked like it was stripped for parts and dumped.

During the third week of August, while at home, I was looking through a popular magazine and just happened to see a picture of an old car that seemed very similar to the car we had seen near Milepost 229. Taking the magazine to work the next day, I showed the picture to Dan Messaros. The photo was of a 1931 Ford Model A sedan. We both agreed that the car in the lake and the picture in the magazine were the same model of Ford. After seeing Mr. Frick's 1927 Chevy, receiving Dr. York's report, and our thoughts regarding the picture in the magazine, we knew that the car we had seen in the lake was not the Warren's.

In September, we conducted a few more dives near the south shore roadway looking for a place that dropped off very quickly near the road. We dove at a site named LaPoel Day Use Area about two miles east of Fairholm. Although LaPoel did have some dramatic drop-offs, it was not near the old Olympic Highway and did not exhibit a "*little curve in the highway*". La Poel Day Use Area was certainly not the right place, but it was a fun place to dive and full of local history. If the trees at this area could talk, I imagine they would tell a few very interesting tales.

The Arcadia Resort access road under the sign led travelers to the Resort and the shores of Lake Crescent. The area is now named LaPoel. Years ago, the buildings were removed. Now it is a simple day use picnic area. This area is two miles east of Fairholm on the south shore of the Lake. The Warrens would have driven on this section of the Olympic Highway and beyond for another ½ mile before meeting their end on July 3, 1929. The photo was taken from the Olympic Highway looking west. Courtesy of Olympic National Park.

Lake Crescent from the top of Mount Storm King looking toward Fairholm and the far west end of the Lake. Barnes Point is at the bottom of the picture and Log Cabin Resort is to the lower far right out of the picture. Ambulance Point or Meldrim Point (Madrona Point) can be seen as a prominent point on the left side ¾ of the way up the lake. Courtesy of Olympic National Park.

We did another exploration dive at Milepost 226. This section of road was on a large sweeping curve. and was certainly not *" a little curve in the highway."* We found that the underwater terrain dropped off rapidly. Our divers could see clearly that the old road bed was at one time next to the water and that it was now elevated as much as 10 feet above the water. This was the wrong place too but could have been the spot where the sailor Curtis Thompson reported seeing a Roadster go into the lake so many years ago.

We needed to keep in mind the road had been improved many times since 1929. The turnouts seen along the road today were sharp curves in the road years ago. The road had been straightened as well as

The Olympic Highway looking west as it curves around Lake Crescent. This view is of the east end of the lake between present day Govin's Hill and Sledgehammer Point. Photo is circa 1928. Note the narrow gravel road, concrete cribbing to support the road and wooden guardrail. The Warrens would have driven their 1927 Chevrolet sedan on this section of road traveling west. Note the mountain peak in the distance at the head of Barnes Creek. Courtesy of Olympic National Park.

elevated, leveled, and armored to prevent waves from washing it out. Guardrails were added to curves with a history of cars going into the lake. We needed to think about what the road would have looked like in 1929. We researchers old pictures and found the early roads to be dusty, narrow, and surfaced with basalt gravel that could cut tires to ribbons. The road was a challenge to negotiate for even the best of drivers back then.

OLYMPIC HIGHWAY
- LAKE CRESCENT-

The Olympic Highway from Govin's Hill looking west toward the Lake. The area is also known to be part of the ancient landslide that occurred about 6,000 years ago. The steep cliff face to the left and to the right of the roadway is part of that landslide. The Warrens would have driven their 1927 Chevy on this section of road traveling west. Courtesy of Olympic National Park.

We needed to find the exact location Sheriff Pike had described in the 1929 newspaper articles. We needed to find a *"little curve in the highway."*

In early October, I called Bill Walker and told him about the Warren case. According to Bud Gray, Bill had knowledge of many underwater features of Lake Crescent. He had already heard the Warren story from Bud who had telephoned him earlier the previous month. While talking with Walker, it suddenly occurred to me we had talked one year earlier, when he called the Storm King Ranger Station to inquire about a rumor he had heard of an airplane that sank in the Lake near the Lake Crescent Lodge. Supposedly, the aircraft was on floats and landed near the Lodge. Apparently, when a boat went out to meet the plane to transport passengers to shore, the boat accidentally punctured a pontoon on the plane which quickly filled with water, taking the plane to the bottom of the lake. I had never heard this story before, and it was memorable enough and probably recent enough that if it had actually happened, it would be a very well-known story, even to me. There had been a regulation in place for many years prohibiting float planes from landing on the Lake which raised my doubts about the validity of the story. The lake in question was probably not Lake Crescent.

Bill told me a story about a dive he had done 12 or 13 years prior in which he found an old car. He said he would be happy to show Dan Messaros and me the location. Bill thought this car might be the Warren car. The car had wheels and was sitting on its side in about 60 feet of water, in a cove, near a waterfall, at the far eastern end of the lake. The problem I had with the site was is it didn't even come close to the site described by Sheriff Pike. This spot was ten miles east of the west end of the lake. A date of November 11 was decided upon to dive this site known as Pirates Cove. I called Bud Gray to make sure he was invited. He and photographer John Rawlings would be joining the effort. I was very excited to be able to dive with these professionals.

On November 11, we all assembled at the dive locker at Lake Crescent in the early morning. The weather was cool with overcast skies and intermittent rain showers. Dan Messaros was teamed with Lynn Roberson. I was with Bill Walker and Bud Gray and John Rawlings were a team. Messaros and I were wearing full face masks equipped with voice communications. We split the search area into two parts, east and west, divided by the water fall. Messaros' team found the car in 65 feet of water a short distance west of the waterfall and asked to have the teams converged at the wreck site. The wrecked car had nearly disintegrated, partially buried in mud and rocks and was covered with rust. One door was exposed along with a small piece of the hood. John Rawlings and I photographed and videotaped what we could see of the car. It appeared to be of the same vintage and make as the car found near the Rock Screen near Milepost 229, meaning this was not likely the Warren car either. However, what were these two wrecked and stripped old cars even doing in the lake? We took measurements and compared them to the auto at the Rock Screen and concluded the car in Pirates Cove and the one at the Rock Screen were the same model and likely the same year. They were both Ford Model A's.

Late in the day on November 11, 2001, I received a radio report from Park Dispatch that two men were overdue from a hike into the mountains on the ridges south of Lake Crescent. I telephoned the reporting party, the wife of one of the missing men and discovered that the two hikers were in their early 70's. She said they were trying to find and hike some of the World War II lookout tower trails in the park. They had picked an abandoned trail on the west end of Lake Crescent that ascended to Aurora Ridge, the ridge that separates the Lake Crescent Valley from the Sol Duc Valley. We had a series of historic maps in the Storm King Ranger Station map case just these kinds of incidents.

Months ago, when I first heard the name Madrona Point, the location Sheriff Pike had described in 1929, I looked in this very map case to find an old map of the Lake. There were indeed various old maps of the Lake but nothing that seemed old enough. However, I should have looked a bit closer. The map I found in this case would bust the Warren investigation wide open!

While gearing up for a possible night search and rescue mission, I pulled several maps of the Lake out of the case. One appeared to be old and was drawn in pencil. It looked just like the kind map I needed to familiarize myself with some of the old trails. It was on paper that was yellow-brown and a bit brittle from age. I found the old trails I was looking for and began to formulate a plan to send a few Rangers up the old trail to hastily search the area, looking for clues of the overdue hikers. I also pulled out a new customized topographic map that showed our current park trails. We would need to use these to access the search area and to set up containment of the probable search area. The first thing to do after taking the initial report and assessing the situation of a missing person in the wilderness is set up containment of the search area, so that if the person or persons missing should walk out of the wilderness, we would know about it.. It also makes the search area a lot smaller, increasing the likelihood of finding them. Our urgency in this incident was high due to the fact these two hikers were not prepared to spend the night in the wilderness, were in terrain that they were unfamiliar with, and most importantly the weather was cold with occasional rain showers and heavy rain predicted for the next day.

I was the Incident Commander (IC) for this search. What the IC does during the first 24 hours of a search could have a significant affect on the outcome of the mission. It's important that things be done right in order to avoid long, extended searches. Search missions are treated as an emergency and a quick response is necessary to preserve clues and find the missing person before they can get into any further trouble.

But, back to the penciled in, yellow-brown map! A closer look at the map revealed that it was indeed traced. The original map used to make this traced map must have been produced before Olympic National Park was formed in 1938. Several of the features on it were clearly titled with different names than those of a modern map of the Lake. The old map covered most of Lake Crescent and showed all of the prominent points.

I compared the old map to a USGS topographic 7.5-minute map of the same general area. They appeared to be of the same scale with the same size township and range lines. I saw the name Meldrim Point on the old map and then saw another name next to it in parenthesis, *Madrona.* I was stunned. I had just found a map that told me exactly were Madrona Point was and would provide us with our best clue. Our chances of finding the Warren car, and perhaps even Blanche and Russell Warren, increased significantly.

A section of the old map of Lake Crescent. Note the words Madrona in parenthesis next to the work Meldrim Pt. This appears to be a hand drawn tracing of an early topographic map dated to about 1930. The original map is in the park archives. Courtesy of Olympic National Park

Later that night, the overdue hikers walked out, cold, wet but otherwise uninjured. They had indeed gotten lost but found the way back to their car by following terrain features flowing toward the lake and highway. The off trail terrain they were in was some of the roughest on the Olympic Peninsula.

I telephoned Bob Caso, who, up to this point, had been showing me bathometric maps of the Lake, trying to find the right topography of places that could be Madrona Point. I told him about finding the map. He suggested we compare the one I had found with his barometric map. I visited Bob at his home in Port Angeles that night and showed him my prize map. He was quite surprised and excited over the find of this old map. He said more than once that evening while examining the map, "Oh my!" in his New Jersey accent.

It was now time to focus our efforts on the area around the newly found Madrona Point. I phoned Bill Walker and asked if he would be willing to come to Lake Crescent on the weekend of November 18, my day off, and dive Madrona Point. I explained to him how I found the map and how it pinpointed the area we needed to search. The date was agreed upon. We would once again dive Ambulance, Meldrim or Madrona Point, a place we now knew was only one place, but this time with a new focus and objective. This new objective was to find the underwater topography that Sheriff Pike described 72 years earlier, the same location Pike's investigators found all the clues. I felt confident this new piece of information would lead our team to a successful conclusion.

Toward the end of the second week of November, I started to get phone calls from a number of local and regional newspapers and television stations. The Park Information Officer (PIO), Barb Maynes, handled the bulk of these providing pictures and video we had taken of the Ford Model A sedans. In the November 13, edition of the *Peninsula Daily News*, a story about our car discoveries and our search for the Warren's ran on the front page, written by Brian Gawley. They used video we had shot of the Ford Model A at Pirates Cove and cut a few digital still photos out of it. *Port Angeles Television Productions* and *Peninsula Cable News Network* both ran stories about the search for the Warrens.

Also, during the week of November 13, Kristin Dizon of the *Seattle Post-Intelligencer* called several times, requesting an interview with me. She was very interested in coming to Lake Crescent to write a story about the search for the Warrens. I was excited to have her write it, because she would reach a very large regional audience. The next week, a front- page article appeared in the paper. Ms. Dizon did a wonderful job telling the Warren story. During interviews with Ms. Dizon, I had asked her if she would help find relatives of the Warren family. The story was also picked up by the *Associated Press* and by many local regional and national newspapers. The *Aberdeen Daily World* ran the story a few days after the *Seattle Post-Intelligencer* story.

A few days after the stories began appearing, I received an email from the park's A ssistant S uperintendent, Roger Rudolph, who said he had received a phone call from a man from Joyce, Washington, a small town about five miles north and east of Lake Crescent. The man told Roger that the 1931 Ford Model A cars we had found were related to a gang of car thefts from the early 1930s. Four local men were arrested in about 1933 and charged with stealing cars and stripping them for parts. Apparently, parts were hard to find in the 1930s, and a car was more valuable for them than keeping and selling the whole car. The man further stated that the shell of the car, having been stripped, was pushed into Lake Crescent. This explained the two Ford Model A cars in the lake and their condition. Crime was alive and well banc then. More importantly, it appeared that the tactic of using the media to reach out to the public was going to provide some valuable clues. Sheriff Pike had done the same thing in 1929, and now it appeared the tactic was working for me.

On November 18, Bill Walker, his son Joe, and I conducted a scuba dive survey of an area from Eagle Point (about three-fourths of a mile east of Fairholm) to a point a few hundred feet west of La Poel, about two miles east of Fairholm. This would be a search of about 1.25 miles, all underwater. We decided on a maximum depth of sixty feet. We used underwater scooters owned by Bill, that would propel us through the water much faster than swimming with fins. If we calculated correctly, this survey would take us over the very spot Harry Brooks and Sheriff Pike found clues in 1929. Bill and Joe splashed first, and I conducted the surface-support function.

When the Walkers surfaced east of Cross Creek (a small creek about 400 feet east of the Meldrim Point), they reported seeing very steep underwater terrain about 250 feet east of Meldrim Point. They saw what appeared to be a circular hole about 12 feet across at the top of a cliff about 40 feet deep. Later in the morning, I dove with Bill and the scooters and saw the top of the circular hole he and Joe had found the previous dive. We surfaced and saw that the hole was about thirty feet from the edge of the old road bed and next to a *"little curve in the highway."* We also saw an old Madrona tree on the opposite side of the road. The hole, plus the sharp drop that, from the roadway, *"sloped downward to an undetermined depth where the water is deep blue and the bottom cannot be seen,"* sent a chill up and down my spine. There was also a narrow shelf next to the road before the underwater terrain dropped off sharply. The location was about fifty feet west of the Milepost Marker 223 of Highway 101. All of this matched perfectly with Sherriff Pike's description in the Port Angeles Evening News newspaper article of August 17, 1929. Bill, Joe, and I all believed we had found the exact spot where Sheriff Pike and Harry Brooks discovered evidence of the Warrens so many years before.

As soon as I was able to get back to the Ranger Station, I briefed Dan Messaros about our dive. I told him that we were going to dive the site again the very next weekend, searching the hole we found in hopes of finding additional clues. If a car had somehow had fallen into that hole, there didn't appear to be anything to stop it from descending a long way down, however deep that might be. A car falling into that hole would be an incredible stroke of bad luck when terrain east and west of the hole would likely hang up a vehicle not allowing it to free fall into very deep water.

Later in the afternoon, I heard Kristin Dizon from the *Seattle Post-Intelligencer*. She told me that she had received a call from a woman in Aberdeen, Washington, who stated she was a relative of the Warrens. Kristin gave me her number and soon I was connected to Anne

Klein, Charles Warren's cousin. She was stunned to read an article in the *Aberdeen World* newspaper about her long, lost relatives. Anne said she knew the story of Blanche and Russell's mysterious disappearance in 1929, having heard the story from Warren family members. I asked if the two sons, Frank and Charles Warren were still alive. Both, she said had died many years before. She added that Charles had children and that she would help me contact them. She told me that Charles Warren had a daughter who lived in Oklahoma, Patricia Smith (Warren). Charles' other children were Roland (Rollie) from Oak Harbor, Washington, and Phoebe Bardin (Warren), who lived in California. Anne provided me with a phone number for Patricia.

I called Patricia that very afternoon. I introduced myself, but she already knew who I was and was expecting my call. Patricia was very excited and thrilled. Anne Klein had already called to tell her about our search efforts and the newspaper stories. She said her brother, Roland (Rollie), was living in Oak Harbor on Whidbey Island in Washington State. That was not very far from Lake Crescent! I go his phone number. It was thrilling to talk to family members and blood relatives of the missing couple.. When I called Bob Caso later that day to tell him of the information, Bob was absolutely stunned. Once again, he said, "Oh, my!" We were making good progress!

The next day, I called Roland Warren. Rollie, as his family called him, said his father, Charles, had told him many years ago, about how his parents had disappeared while coming home on July 3, 1929. Rollie said that his father never talked much about the incident, probably because his father was young at the time and many years had gone by since they disappeared. Out of courtesy and a sense of protocol, I asked Rollie for permission to allow the Olympic National Park dive team to pursue the case. I told him about the evidence we had found so far and about Bob Caso. He had an elderly aunt named Louise Allen who lived in Port Angeles and she knew his father Charles, as well as Blanche and Russell. He was uncertain of her health however. I told Rollie we were planning to dive on November 25 at Ambulance Point (Madrona Point). Rollie indicated he wanted to bring his family to the Lake to meet the divers. He had family visiting the week of the Thanksgiving holiday but would bring his family to the Lake on Saturday December 8, two weekends after Thanksgiving. Finding the Warren family and having a good conversation with them was a very positive step. Support from the Warrens was critical to a successful outcome.

On Sunday, November 25, the weather was cold with a light cloud cover and a bit of snow flying in the air. It was near-perfect weather for a dive at Madrona Point to confirm we were searching a high-probability area. Dan Messaros and I had not gone to great depths near the "hole," and we felt this diving deep into and around the "hole " would help us plan future dives. We piled on a few extra layers of insulation under our dry suits to protect us from the cold water and air. We all laughed at the idea we'd be diving in a snowstorm. When planning dive operations with boats, the weather is an important factor when anchoring , when enter the water, and when divers get back into the boat. Needless to say, calm winds and calm seas make dive operations much easier.

Kristin Dizon of the *Seattle Post-Intelligencer* was aboard our vessel, as was Dennis Brag of *Peninsula News Network*. Dan and I splashed together at about 11:00 a.m. and submerged about 100 feet east of the point within the small cove and just west of the "hole." We swam in an easterly direction at a depth of 100 feet, following the edge of a very steep cliff. We could not see the bottom of the wall as we swam along, so we were not sure how high the cliff was. The water was a cool 43 degrees below the thermocline, a level in the water column were near-surface warm water sits on top of deeper cold water. That level was at the 60 foot depth. Visibility was very respectable 60 feet.

The lake was beginning its seasonal 'turn over'. Lakes are said to 'turn over' every fall and spring as the temperatures change. When the air temperature cools off in the fall, the water also cools finding equilibrium with the air. The cooling water condenses and becomes heavier, sinking. Warmer water near the shore moves in to try to replace the sinking cooler water, thus creating micro-currents.

When Dan and I surfaced, we came up near the *"little curve in the highway."* That the dive team had now surveyed most of the area shallower than 60 feet and above the edge of the cliff suggesting the car was probably in very deep water over the edge of the cliff. It was clear the Warren car was not in shallow water, for if it was, Sheriff Pike's investigators would have seen it 1929 and they would have easily closed the case. There should be a trail of debris on the Lake bottom, the car spilling its contents as it turned over in its descended into the abyss. The washing machine and groceries Russell had purchased on July 3rd , if we could find evidence, would be a very good clues. Car owners in 1929 usually carried roadside tools, a tire-patch kit, air pump, and other tools to make repairs would also be very good clues. They would tell us the path the Chevy took.

We decided that a team of divers should search the area very closely, since the clues from the car accident over 72 years ago would be very hard to find. We agreed that a close grid search starting near the shoreline would give us our best chance of finding clues. We all agreed that finding and following the clues was going to lead us to something significant, hopefully the remains of Blanche and Russell.

We had a list of the items supposedly in the car.

- A washing machine
- $100 worth of groceries
- Clothing and personal items in two suitcases from Blanche's stay at the hospital
- A second sun visor
- A second flower vase

All those groceries must have been quite a haul. One hundred dollars was a lot of money in 1929 and would have bought a lot of groceries. The brand of washing machine was unknown to us but it would surely be obvious to us, should we be lucky enough to find it.

A question that puzzled us all was, where do you put a washing machine in a two-door sedan? Did they tie it to the back of the car, perhaps using the fender as support? Perhaps it wasn't the sedan we envisioned but rather a Chevrolet truck. With all this stuff in the car, there just had to be clues lying on the bottom of that Lake that would lead us to the car.

On the following weekend of December 2, Park divers Paul Seyler, Dan Messaros, and I, plus volunteers Bill and Joe Walker, plunged into the cold and clear waters of Lake Crescent at Madrona Point with a plan to search the area near the hole at the edge of the cliff. Our plan was to move very slowly, looking for any objects on the list of clues. We began just west of the *little curve in the highway*, thinking the car was traveling in a westerly direction and that momentum would carry it a few feet west of the curve where we suspected it left the road. We departed the surface near shore beginning our descent into the depths in hopes of finding clues and maybe even the car. The water and weather conditions had not changed since the week before and fortunately, visibility was still a respectable 60 feet.

The challenge of these dives and the ones to come in deeper and deeper water, was to manage the amount of risk. Bob Caso had said he and the NEMGORF dive club stopped diving in the area of Ambulance Point because the water was too deep and they *were going to die* if they went any deeper. Up to this point, we had stayed above 130 feet in depth within the no-decompression-limits. At 60 feet, a diver has about 55 minutes of bottom time before the bodies tissues become oversaturated with nitrogen (the air you breath is 21% oxygen, 78% nitrogen and 1% inert gases like helium) requiring off gassing (decompression) stops before surfacing. If a diver comes to the surface too quickly after having spent time at depth, the nitrogen comes out the tissues too fast causing a serious medical issue. At 120 feet, the diver has about ten minutes of bottom time.

One of the safety factors in single tank diving is that an 80 cubic foot scuba cylinder, by far the most common size, will hold just about the right amount of air for divers who wish to stay within the no-decompression limit. We were all diving with single tanks and large pony bottles as a backup air source. We were also diving with oxygen-enriched air or Nitrox at 28 percent, 32 percent and 36 percent blends. This gas replaced some of the nitrogen in the tank with oxygen, thereby reducing the amount of nitrogen absorption, a critical factor for avoiding complications such as the "bends". We also hung extra cylinders of Nitrox with attached regulators from lines off the side of the boat at depths of 20, 60 , and 100 feet, just in case someone had an equipment malfunction.

Further compounding the risk was both the cold water and steep terrain with loose rocks everywhere. A slight nudge of a rock in the wrong place would send it silently screaming down the cliff. When underwater, you can't exactly shout to your buddy below to look out for a falling rock. The diving was getting more difficult and complicated, requiring more planning and detail. Luckily, Dan Messaros had recently completed a Dive Master Course, and I was a Master Diver with over 1,700 dives and a high level of skill in deep lakes, swift water rivers, high altitude, and the ocean.

The Walkers were also Advanced Divers and had commensurate experience. Bill started in 1967 and had over 3,000 thousand dives, many of them solo dives. He had excellent control of his buoyancy and showed a special calmness underwater. I wasn't worried about our National Park Service divers, but I was worried about our VIP (volunteer) divers. Placing a volunteer in a high-risk operation was something I had to think about very carefully. We had to find ways to minimize the risks.

I had helped train nearly all the Park divers on our team and felt comfortable with them. I knew what standard (NAUI - National Association of Underwater Instructors) they had been trained and certified and felt they were all well trained. All that being said, we were hoping that we would find the car and the Warrens at a depth no greater than 150 feet.

As the team moved from the narrow shelf near shore toward the deeper water, it looked like our clue-detection plan was going to work. We began to find all sorts of old objects from vehicle wrecks in the past. The problem was not a lack of evidence, but too much evidence. How do we sort them all out? I gave each diver instructions not to remove anything. Instead, they were to mark the evidence with a piece of flagging or a Pelican buoy (a small float).

At about 30 feet deep, I saw Joe swim toward a small object and inspect it. I saw him mark the object. We continued to swim further down and eventually along the edge of the hole in the cliff. The hole extended down to about 100 feet in depth and then dropped off a sharp cliff. If a diver stayed within the walls of the hole and follow it down into the abyss, was like a waterslide. Bill Walker thought it was an ancient waterfall.. When the lake was 80 feet lower, 6,000 years ago, this hole and slide would have been above the ancient shoreline. It certainly looked like a waterfall. The hole at the top of the cliff wasn't really a hole but half-moon shaped and carved out section of the cliff face. I saw Bill Walker descend down the slide. Joe and I followed him, descending slowly, looking for clues and evidence.

From above, I saw Bill direct his son's attention to a location in the slide at about 70 feet in depth. He picked up a black object, examined it for several minutes, and then returned it to its original location. Bill marked the spot. We reached the 100 depth and turned our attention toward the west where Dan Messaros and Paul Seyler (of the Olympic National Park Maintenance Division) were. They were heading west and into shallower water. Bill, Joe and I slowly followed them. After making our required 3 minute safety stop at 15 feet, we all surfaced.

We were all now at the surface about fifty feet east of the Point and near the beach. Paul Seyler told me that he saw what looked like a trash can lid near the edge of a steep cliff in about 90 feet of water. Dan Messaros thought that it could be a clue, perhaps an object from the Warren car. Bill Walker reported that the black object he picked up looked like a flower vase, an important clue on our list. . Dan Messaros and I decided to return to the site where Paul Seyler had found the round disk, so we could take a closer look.

The round disk was teetering on the edge of the cliff and could have easily fallen into the abyss, never to be found. We were lucky. Bill and Joe also returned to the slide and retrieved the black vase. We were all back at the beach at Madrona Point in about 15 minutes.

Dan and I took the metal disk out of the water at the beach and saw that it certainly was not a trash can lid, at least not one I had ever seen. What it looked like was the lid of a washing machine. I had seen ones similar to this as a child at our family summer camp in Maine. Bill Walker showed us the black vase, and it indeed did look like the kind of vase that could be used inside an automobile. It appeared to have the pedestal base broken off perhaps to fit into the car mounted vase holder.

The flower vase found by the Walkers. The bottom of the pedestal appears to be missing. Courtesy of the Olympic National Park.

The washing machine lid found by Paul Seyler and Dan Messaros in a water depth of about 90 feet of water. The black knob had a faint outline of the letter "N" indicating that the machine was manufactured by Norge. Courtesy of Olympic National Park.

When we all got back to the dive locker at Barnes Point, we secured the black vase as evidence and stored the washing machine lid in actual Lake Crescent water inside the wet boat bay. We were concerned that if we exposed it to air for very long, it would begin to rust and deteriorate. I called the National Park Service Cultural Resource Conservation Center. Stephanie Toothman told me that the best solution for short term preservation was to store the lid in the waters of Lake Crescent to reduce the amount oxidation that the lid would be exposed to. We took pictures of the lid and the vase and examined them carefully to try to ascertain their age and connect them to the Warren case.

The washing machine lid was the piece of evidence that created the most excitement. We all knew the Warrens had bought a washing machine on the day they disappeared, and here was an old washing machine lid in our hands from a place known as Madrona Point. We felt the chances were very high the washer lid was from the Warren car. Still, being good investigators, we felt it was worth a few extra steps to evaluate it to prove that it belonged to the Warren washing machine, thereby precluding with a high degree of certainty that the whole story of the disappearance of the Warrens 72 years prior was all true and we were searching in the right place.

An Internet search of antique washing machines revealed an site named *Oldwasher.com* and was an online museum of old washing machines. I saw an e-mail address and a contact phone number for the website. I sent an e-mail to the museum with a written narrative of our dive project and attached pictures of the washer lid. I also called the contact number and left a message on the museum voice mail machine.

The next day, I received a reply from the museum and spoke to the owner. He would search his records and inventory for a lid similar to the photo I had sent to him. A few days later, he sent me some drawings of a washing machine manufactured by Norge built in the late 1920's. One drawing showed a washing machine lid that was identical to the one we found in the lake.

Bill Walker, always the inquisitive person, took a closer look at the lid's black knob and saw there was an outline of a letter N on the top. The fact that he is color blind aided him in seeing the N, a clue I had missed when I examined it. The N was manufactured onto the knob and strongly suggested the lid was manufactured by Norge.

I was now convinced the lid was from the Warren car. Here was the first piece of physical evidence since Sheriff Pike had suspended his investigation in September 1929 that could, with a high degree of certainty, link us directly to the Warrens and possibly tell us where the car was.

The flower vase was made of dense, thick, glossy black glass. It was heavy for a vase and looked and felt like the rock substance known as Obsidian. Another Internet search, this time for car flower vases, showed that most vases were very fancy with a great deal of ornamentation. Most of the vases I saw on the websites were clear crystal or ivory white. I could not find any black, plain vases. Surprisingly, I talked to a car vase collector who lived in Port Angeles. He doubted what we found was actually a car vase since it was so plain and ordinary. The Warren car did have flower vases mounted inside as reported in the 1929 newspaper articles and stated that one was found by Sheriff Pike's investigative team. Unfortunately, no description was offered of the vase. Could this vase be from the Warren car? Or maybe it had been thrown into the lake at a later date, perhaps by a family member to memorialize the missing Warrens.

We needed to know if the vase actually used by the Warrens in their car. The biggest clue was at the bottom of the vase. It was likely designed to stand on its own but the base appeared to be broken off. For this vase to fit into a metal bracket inside the car, the pedestal base, larger in diameter than the middle of the vase, had to be removed. Russell or perhaps the previous owner could have knocked off the base. The neck was thick glass and very rugged requiring a fair amount of force to break it. It looked old and exhibited a mold seam. We estimated the vase to be between 75 and 100 years old. Due to its proximity to the debris trail and the other physical evidence, we concluded it was most likely from Blanche and Russell Warren's 1927 Chevrolet.

The trail to the Warren's Chevrolet sedan was getting hot. The clues we had found so far were substantial and compelling. Over the next few days, I was able to gain needed and much welcomed access to old newspaper articles stored at the Clallam County Historical Society from June, July, August and September of 1929. While searching them, I found a Montgomery Ward Store in Port Angeles in 1929 that sold Norge washing machines and appliances. Perhaps they bought it at Montgomery Ward. I couldn't wait to tell Bob Caso what we had found. I was anxious to see his face when we told him about the washing machine lid and flower vase.

That evening, I visited with Bob as his home. I sat in his living room and calmly told him we had found what I believed were significant clues. He comment was "Oh my God." He was stunned.

Spurred by our recent discoveries, Bill Walker, Joe Walker, Dan and I teamed up to further search the *"little curve in the highway."* On December 9, the water was clear and cold with about 80 feet of visibility. We were confident there had to be other clues near the shoreline but in deeper water. The area appeared to be littered with old car parts and evidence of other incidents from years past.

The question was how many more clues had survived the 72 years since the Warrens had mysteriously disappeared. Road construction and a seemingly long list of accidents in the past suggested evidence could still be in the water. The challenge would be to determine which clues would be part of the Warren case. To mark the location of each clue, we brought wired tags, like in previous dives, to mark the location of clues we found.

On the day of our dive, Charles Warren's son Rollie and his wife Geneil, daughter Kristine, and two year old grandson Nicholas, arrived at the Lake Crescent dive locker. I was anxious to meet the Warrens, especially Rollie, and shake the hand of a Warren family member for the first time. I showed Rollie and his family the Norge washing machine lid. I explained that we felt it was the first tangible piece of evidence that we had found that confirmed his grandparents' disappearance. To think that Rollie's grandfather might have actually handled the washing machine lid 72 years ago was truly stunning.

I wondered what Rollie and Geneil were now thinking. Kristine was in her early 30's and had strikingly similar facial characteristic to her great-grandmother Blanche and her great-great-grandmother, Bertha Matteson. She was an attractive woman. Young Nicholas seemed very curious and I doubt if he had ever seen a scuba diver before. Geneil was all smiles and offered her family's full support for the investigation that still lay ahead. She presented me with a three-ring binder that was full of family pictures. I was able to see a wedding picture of Blanche and Russell for the first time. I was finally getting to know Blanche and Russell Warren.

Dan Messaros and I plunged first and already having decided to search the deeper waters. Bill and Joe Walker, the father-and-son team, found a tire and an air pump of similar size and construction that could have been used on a 1927 Chevy. Joe also found a wooden apple box with intact glass Mason canning jars in it and a glass bottle of White Ace Shoe Polish. The lids of the mason jars had long since rusted away and whatever contain they had was gone. Could these have been some of the groceries that Russell Warren bought while in Port Angeles on July 3, 1929?

The Warren family, Rollie, Geneil, Kristine, and little Nicholas were waiting for us on the beach with warm drinks and kind smiles. We brought these clues to the surface and secured them as evidence.

The shoe polish bottle was familiar to Bill Walker, an avid bottle collector. After a bit of research, he determined it appeared to be about 75 years old. Its relationship to the other objects in the wooden box placed it squarely within the time frame of the 1920s. Now that we had a an increasing body of evidence, it was time to plot them on a map that would hopefully reveal a debris trail. With luck, we'd find the car at the end of it. We knew the path we had seen so far led to much deeper water, and that worried me a great deal. The deep water would dramatically increase the risks to our dive team.

On December 16, Dan Messaros and I, along with Paul Seyler and Bill Walker, plunged into the lake again. The water was clear and cold, and there were a few inches of fresh snow in the surrounding mountains. At out location, the air was cold enough that it snowed during the day. We invited Kristin Dizon and a few other newspaper and TV media people to the dive operation. As we had been doing all along, our mission was to search for further evidence, and if we were lucky enough to find the 1927 Chevy or human remains, we'd have plenty of witnesses to record the event. On this dive we planned to follow the debris trail over the edge of the cliff and down the wall to the bottom, if possible. Sonar soundings from the park boat indicated the bottom of the cliff was at about 160 feet.

We reached a depth of 90 feet, the edge of the vertical cliff and pitched ourselves over the lip descend down the wall. It was pitch black below and the bottom was not visible. As we approached 130 feet, the bottom began to appear. The sonar was right, it appeared to be at about 160 feet in depth. From there, a gravelly bottom sloped in a 45 degree angle, similar to the shallow areas above. We saw the large hole (or waterfall) off to our east that terminated at to the bottom of the wall. This was the same hole where the black flower vase was found and it was within the area we considered to be the debris trail.

Our bottom time was very short, a mere 10 minutes. We leveled off at 130, and stayed at that depth while searching the wall and the bottom 30 feet below. As we ascended, we searched the wall below the spot where we had found the washing machine lid. We surfaced after about 40 minutes, spending about 20 minutes at 30 feet, still within the no-decompression limit. We made a safety stop at 15 feet breathing a mix of Nitrox 36 from our staged scuba cylinders. We didn't find any new physical evidence, but we did gather good knowledge of the terrain.

However, Bill did see several large fish (trout) on this dive and noticed they showed scratch marks on their sides. He thought the fish habitat could be inside something that had sharp metal or glass. Maybe the 1927 Chevy was nearby and the fish had been swimming in it.

On January 13, 2002, after a holiday break, we planned to go to a depth of 150 feet and close to the bottom of the wall to search the area east and west of where we stopped at our last dive. By now, we had made about 10 dives each to the 130 foot level to maintain depth rating. We started building a whole lot more planning into each dive and were now hanging scuba cylinders of Nitrox and compressed air at 15 feet, 60 feet, and 90 feet in depth to build more safety into our operations. We were also diving with large pony cylinders with an extra regulator hanging from them. These would allow us to reach the surface in the event of a catastrophic main air cylinder or regulator failure. We were still diving within the no-decompression limits, which meant that our bottom time was less than ten minutes. That's not a lot to search such a wide area.

We each carried two flashlights due to the sometimes less-than-clear water. We figured the visibility at depth might be limited due to the angle of the sun at this time of year and the fact that we had considerable rain and snow since our last dive in December, which would cloud up the water. We had hoped that the water would be clear at depth. The lake was likely turning over again, which would make the visibility and clarity undesirable.

The plan was to dive to the base of the cliff at 150 feet, and then we would split up for a 4 minute swim. I would go west and Dan would go east, then turn around and meet back at our rendezvous point. We departed the surface with the idea that our plan was solid, even though we were going to split up for a few minutes at depth.

Our descent down the wall to the 150-foot depth went without incident, and we arrived feeling good, although we could both feel the strong effects of nitrogen narcosis. All the previous dives to 130 feet were excellent training for both of us to deal with the narcosis. Dan and I checked each other's flashlights and then departed to our assigned direction; I swam west and Dan swam east. The visibility was very disappointing. I swam west for about two minutes and decided the visibility was just too poor to effectively search the area. I turned around and swam back to the rendezvous stop. I had been gone no more than four minutes total. I shined my flashlight toward the east hoping to see Dan's flashlight approaching. I didn't see anything but the wall next to me and black inky water ahead. I waited for another minute and saw with great relief, the faint light of Dan's flashlight coming in my direction. I signaled him with my flashlight. We gave each other the OK signal, pointed to the surface, and began our ascent toward light and life. We had not found the 1927 Chevy that we were hoping would be within the beams of our flashlights.

When we surfaced, Dan told me he had seen a large square-looking object off in the distance at the place he turned around. He wasn't able to identify what he had seen but felt a return to the spot was needed. Surely we must be very close. Perhaps we weren't worthy of finding the car just yet.

On March 24, Dan and I dove to 150 feet again, following the debris trail marked with flagging we had set up months before. We hoped that the visibility would improve so that we could effectively search the base of the wall toward the west, and if time permitted, toward the east and the place Dan Messaros turned around at the sight of a square object. This time we were going to stay together. We followed the wall down to 150 feet and arrived feeling good. We could see to depths beyond 175 feet which gave us more than 25 feet of vertical visibility. The better water clarity was aided by the sunlight from above was penetrating to this depth, making the search much easier.

We turned west and followed the wall, hoping to run into the car or the washing machine. We did not find the car or evidence that it had dropped off the cliff in a westerly direction. Our thinking was that the 1927 Chevy was driving in a westerly direction and momentum would have naturally have carried the vehicle from its entry point into the water toward the west. We ran out of bottom time to search toward the east and surfaced without incident and having found nothing new. Sometimes, an absence of clues is a clue in itself. If only we had time to search the area to our east. We'd have to wait until the next dive.

Our next operation would be to look in an easterly direction from the base of the wall. This would return us to the area Dan had thought he saw a square shaped object off in the distance on January 13th. We also discussed the option of waiting another three or four weeks to allow the weather and water to settle, in hopes that visibility and natural light at depth would improve. We were trying to do everything possible to reduce the amount of risk we were taking.

We must be very close to finding something significant.

10

PLENTY OF HELP

Dan Messaros, the other dive team members and I decided to plan a search east of where we had left off. We hoped some new technologies we had recently become aware of would be able to assist us. Our thinking was to use three levels of technology to conduct the search felling this would give us an excellent chance of finding more clues and possibly even the 1927 Chevy. We all agreed that the best layering of technologies would be to first search with side-scan sonar, then if an object of interest was found, run a magnetometer over the area to determine if the object was metal. If it turned out to be a large-sized object, and the side scan sonar image looked promising, then we'd send a Remote Operated Vehicle (ROV) with a video camera down to take a look. We also had two deep-water technical divers on reserve; we had signed them up as volunteers for this one dive operation.

We contacted Gene and Sandra Ralston from Ralston Associates out of Idaho who had done a lot of work with National Park Service divers at Glen Canyon National Recreation Area, which straddles the Arizona, Utah border. Gene had conducted many searches in very deep water at Lake Powell looking for drowning victims, and had considerable experience using side-scan sonar. We briefed him on the type of topography in the Lake at Madrona Point. He stated that he was available and willing to help on April 13.

We also contacted Divers Institute of Technology, a Seattle-based company that specialized in underwater technologies and commercial dive training. They had ROV and a magnetometer that they could bring to the project.

We also contacted Jerome Ryan and John Rawlings. They had been with us on the earlier search for the old car in Pirates Cove that probably was a stolen 1931 Ford Model A sedan. Jerome was a technical dive instructor, and John was working on completing *Extended Range* and *Normoxic Trimix* dive training certifications. John was also a writer and photographer for Advanced Diver Magazine.

Olympic National Park *Archaeologist*, Dave Conca, and the Park *Public Information Officer*, Barb Maynes, were also available on April 13 and were gladly added to the non-diver part of the team. We also invited the local media.

We all agreed that on Saturday, April 13, we would convene and hopefully find the big clues, namely the washing machine, the 1927 Chevy and perhaps Blanche and Russell Warren. On Friday, April 12, Gene and Sandy Ralston arrived with a boat and launched at the Barnes Point boat ramp. I could tell immediately upon meeting Gene and Sandy we were going to get along well and perhaps become lifelong friends. We certainly had much in common. We motored out to the scene of the search and while boating, I gave Gene a briefing of the next day's operation. That evening, Bill Walker, Jerome Ryan, and John Rawlings arrived. Jerome and John stayed at Log Cabin Resort on the eastern shore of the lake.

At 7:00 a.m. the next morning, Saturday, April 13, Bill Walker and I drove out to Lake Crescent on U.S. Highway 101. When we reached the section of the road where the Lake is first visible, we looked toward the far west end of the lake and saw a brilliant rainbow. It was raining on that end of the lake, and with the sun rising in the east; the conditions were perfect for a beautiful, full rainbow. What was even more fascinating was that the rainbow made landfall at Madrona Point and extended over Pyramid Peak. I said, "Look at that Bill. The Warren's must know we're coming to find them. This could be the day!"

At 8:30 a.m., all the team members were present at the Park Dive Locker Barnes Point. The most important person of the day was present, and that was Bob Caso. As I greeted Bob that morning, I couldn't help but think of the work so many people had contributed to try to solve the Warren case over the years. I thought of Sheriff Jack Pike and his efforts 72 years ago, the work of the NEMGORF dive club and of Charles and Frank Warren, who both died without knowing what happened to their parents. But I especially thought of Bob Caso, the death of his beautiful daughter Robin, and how it changed his life. I also wondered what Sheriff Pike would have said to us if he were present on this morning. What would Charles and Frank have said? What would Harry Brooks or Blanches' mother have said? We were following in the footsteps of some very courageous and determined people.

Sheriff Jack Pike had found excellent clues related to the Warren case; clues he believed told the final story. In a few hours, we were going to find out how right Sheriff Pike really was. The Warren family was not present that day, as they had prior commitments and would be present following day.

Three people from the Divers Institute of Technology were also there and were working hard at getting the ROV ready for operation. About 25 people huddled into our little dive locker. I gave everyone a briefing on the day's operation and a strong safety message about dive and boat operations. Dan Messaros was the Dive Officer and he briefed the divers on the plan for the day, which was essentially to standby until a target of interest was identified. This was not the time for accidents. Each working team member was either an official volunteer signed up with Olympic National Park, or they were a paid employee.

At 9:00 a.m., under overcast and partly cloudy skies, with a slight westerly wind, four boats with dive gear and advanced technologies left the docks of Barnes Point and proceeded west to Madrona Point. The water temperature was a cool 46 degrees and it was crystal clear. It looked like the water visibility might be as high as 80 feet. Surface light would easily reach to 150 feet, giving the operation good visibility at depth. The four boats soon arrived at Madrona Point. I was glad to finally start this operation. I had a feeling this was going to be a big day. We had performed a very good search of the area thus far, except for one place directly below and to the east of the "hole."

As the boats settled and anchored into their assigned areas, a few glitches in the new technologies we had along developed and we needed to deal with them. The ROV worked just fine in the water at the dive locker, but once on site at Madrona Point, it refused to work. Two trips to the dive locker at Barnes Point for tools and extra parts did not resolve the issues. Having seen the ROV in operation the evening before, I was convinced this would be a very valuable technology, but only if it would work.

The magnetometer promised by Bob Mester, a Seattle-underwater explorer, failed to show up. So the technologies available to us on this morning were the side-scan sonar and the deep-water divers. Gene Ralston had been operational with the side-scan sonar since about 9:00 a.m. He wanted to get to the site before anyone else arrived, so he could stake out the best location for his boat. The evening before, I had outlined where I wanted him to search as the high-probability area. With the side-scan sonar now being one of two technology options, all eyes were on Gene Ralston as he performed his magic over the next several hours.

At about 2:00 p.m., Gene called me over to his boat stating he wanted me to see some objects that looked interesting. The images on his computer screen were objects detected by the side-scan sonar, and they looked interesting to say the least! He explained to me that one of the objects appeared to have a round, circular appearance at one end. The round part looked too unnatural to have been made by nature. It appeared to be attached to something that was not easily identifiable. Gene could not even begin to guess what it was other than to say that it appeared to be a man-made object. We thought we might be looking at the washing machine. The depth, according to Gene, was a bit over 200 feet.

The object looked like a good candidate for the ROV to examine, if it was operational. Unfortunately, it was still not functioning. The people from Divers Institute of Technology were still trying to make repairs to the unit so I decided to send the deep divers down to identify it. Jerome Ryan and John Rawlings were chomping at the bit to get in the water anyway. Paul Seyler and I helped John and Jerome prepare for the dive, checking cameras, handing gear into the water, and relaying last-minute instructions. I handed John a Pelican Buoy (a Styrofoam float with long rope attached) and asked him to tie it to the washing machine if they found it and send the float to the surface. Bob Caso was aboard my boat and was busy looking over the operation as the divers prepared to enter the water. It must have been a big thrill for Bob. He knew we were close!

At about 3:30 p.m., Jerome and John splashed into the cool and clear waters of Lake Crescent. I was green with envy for not being able to dive with them. I had high hopes that maybe this dive would finally solve the mystery. If only Sheriff Jack Pike had Jerome and John with their technical dive gear in 1929. Prior to the dive, Gene Ralston had set up a small cage of plastic tubing and metal pipe with weights. He placed the cage on the bottom just below the unknown object and attached a rope to a surface float. The divers could now follow the fixed rope to the bottom and swim a short distance to the unidentified object.

As the divers left the surface, we all prayed for their safety and for good results. We watched the bubbles turn from large boiling bubbles indicating the divers were near the surface to small foamy ones indicting they were now in deep water.

Park employee Paul Seyler assisting divers Jerome Ryan (seated) and John Rawlings with gear assembly aboard the park dive boat moments before diving. Note the double tanks, staging tanks and thick, heavy dry suits. Bob Caso, Barb Maynes and the author, Dan Pontbriand were aboard the attached second boat as well as a television camera man. The weather was calm and cool, a perfect day for diving. Strom King Mountain in in the background. Courtesy of Olympic National Park

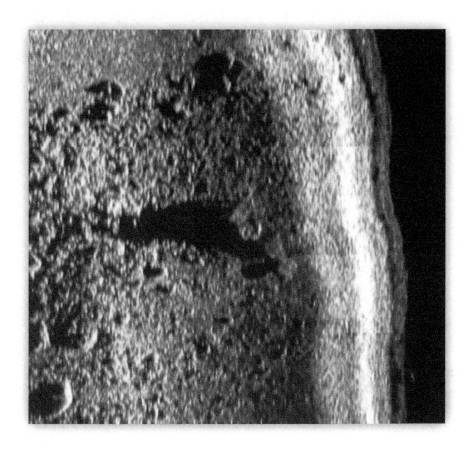

A side-scan sonar image captured by Gene and Sandy Ralston on April 13, 2002 at Madrona Point. The depth is 150 feet at the far left and over 200 feet at the far right of the image. The objects of interest are in the center and near the top of the image. Can you guess what the objects are? Could they be rocks or a stump? Natural or unnatural? The black behind some of the objects are shadows created by the side-scan sonar. Courtesy of Ralston Associates.

As time passed, Bob Caso, Paul Seyler and I kept a steady vigil aboard the park's King Fisher patrol boat, watching bubbles come to the surface. We commented that the bubbles seemed to be stationary and rather small for about ten minutes, which spiked my interest as to what was going on in the depths of the lake. Of course, I was green with envy not being able to dive to that depth, which I believed to be a bit over two hundred feet.

Suddenly, a small yellow buoy popped to the surface. Bob Caso looked at Paul Seyler and said, "What do you think they found?" I looked at the two and said, "I think it must be the washing machine." We waited for another 30 to 40 minutes for the divers to surface, knowing that they had to finish their decompression stops to avoid decompression sickness. It was an agonizing amount of time. I wanted to jump in the lake or send a message slate down on a line. I needed to know! As the project leader and principal investigator, I had a lot at stake. Sheriff Pike must have been in the same position that I was when he sent divers down 72 before this day, looking for the Warren car and the Warrens. I wonder what he must have been thinking; knowing that at times he was so close to solving the mystery, just like I was at this moment.

At about 4:15 p.m., John and Jerome surfaced and John spat out his regulator. He was about 50 feet from the boat where Bob, Paul and I were. I shouted, "Did you find the washing machine?" John replied, "No, we found the car!" Videotaping the event was Port Angeles Television Productions. I looked at Bob Caso standing there with his tweed hat, overcoat, and slight lean forward. Bob asked, "Did he say they found the car?" I replied, "Yes, Bob, we found the car!"

Bob said in hushed voice barely audible, "Oh my God. . . Oh my God, we found the car?"

I said to Bob, "Yes, we've done it!" Bob raised his arms and cheered as if he had just scored a goal in the Stanley Cup finals.

Bob had been searching for the Warrens and the 1927 Chevy on and off for nearly 50 years, and now the most significant clue of all had been found. Bob's long journey was nearly over. All of his diver friends from the past who had helped him search for the car could now rest in peace. I wonder what Sheriff Pike would have said if he was here?

As John Rawlings told it, he and Jerome left the surface and descended into the cold and clear water. Jerome was the first to land near the bottom. As John was nearing Jerome's stopped position, near the bottom of the rope, John looked up the slope a short distance and could clearly see what appeared to be an old car lying on its side. Jerome was in slightly deeper water and did not see it and did not see John swim in that direction. Finally, Jerome looked around to find his dive partner and swam upslope toward John. He must have seen the old car, but John said he pointed to the car. John stated he wanted to scream with joy, but his regulator prohibited that. John said he knew that this was the 1927 Chevy sedan that we had been looking for and that others had been searching for over 50 years. John checked his depth gauge and it read 166 feet. H attached the Pelican Buoy rope to the front bumper of the car and sent buoy to the surface. According to John, he wanted to bolt to the surface to tell those aboard the surface vessels the great news, that the Warren car had been found. But that was not possible. He and Jerome needed to finish their decompression stops to avoid decompression sickness.

Jerome and John were assisted aboard the dive boat. John smiled and said, "Dan, I knew it was the Warren car the minute I saw it. It looked like the pictures and the cars we had seen that were 1927 Chevy's. There is no doubt in my mind we have found the Warren car." I asked John if Blanche and Russell were inside the car. John said, "I didn't see any bones inside the car. The roof is missing and the car is lying on its side."

Gene Ralston could not have been happier. He and his wife, Sandy, were the heroes of the day. It was their work that had pinpointed the Warren car wreck. With all divers and gear aboard and anchors pulled, we headed back to the dive locker and safe harbor. Once there, I immediately called Chief Ranger Curt Sauer and left a phone message for him. I also called Rollie Warren on Whidbey Island and left a phone message, telling them that we had found the 1927 Chevy.

The 1927 Chevy sedan driven by the Warren's laying on its side. The photo was taken in 170 feet of water and about 30 feet east of the car. The grainy photo is a good example of the color and amount of light the divers could actually see. Note the steep slope, rocks and gravel and clear water. The picture was cut from a video image and taken using only ambient light from the surface. Courtesy of Olympic National Park.

That evening, the team celebrated with a few drinks and dinner at a local pub. The celebration needed to be cut short because, the next day, we wanted to do more work to document the find. Plans were made to have John and Jerome dive to the wreck with a digital video camera to record the pristine conditions of the car. Dan Messaros and I would dive next and visit the car only briefly. Jerome would hand the video camera off to me. Dan and I would keep our dive within the no-decompression limit and surface 45 minutes and before Jerome and John. Dan and I would also stay above the car to limit our exposure to depth. The digital video would allow us to look at the car repeatedly in detail to hopefully determine the whereabouts of Russell and Blanche Warren. We also wanted to share the video with the local and regional media who were very interested in the story.

I was extremely concerned about the next day's dives. Many of our team wanted to dive to the Warren car, but few of them had the training, certification, and experience to dive to that depth and safely return to the surface. Dan Messaros and I had to decide who was going to dive to a depth of 160 feet to the car.

That evening, Bill Walker approached me and asked if he and his son Joe could be included in the dive team. I knew they both had depth ratings of 130 feet as open-water divers. I also knew that they had considerable experience diving, with Bill perhaps having more experience than any person alive diving at Lake Crescent. It was with extreme difficulty that I had to tell Bill and Joe they couldn't participate in the dive because they were diving as volunteers, and I simply couldn't accept the risk. We were obligated to keep the volunteers out of dangerous situations as well as make sure they stayed within their levels of training.

Later that night, I was finally able to talk to Rollie Warren by telephone and tell him the big news. I had called and left a message earlier in the evening. I wish I could have seen the look on his face when he heard my voice message. News like this needed to be told regardless of the time of night.

The next day, the Warren family arrived at Lake Crescent around midmorning. It was good to see Rollie and his family and to be able to repeat the good news in person. Local and regional television and newspaper people were there as well. This time, John Rawlings, Jerome Ryan, Dan Messaros and I, were all armed with cameras. Jerome owned a 35 mm underwater camera, and Dan and I had the underwater digital video camera that belonged to the park. The day was clear and cool with a slight surface wind on the lake. The water was clear and rather calm.

As the dive boats approached the site, the small yellow buoy that John tied to the car was still present and gently bobbing on the surface. The *"little curve in the highway"* was in the background of the little yellow buoy. In my mind, it all lined up perfectly. The car plunged over the side of the road into the "hole" and fell to the location directly under the little yellow buoy. Sheriff Pike and his team probably dragged this very spot. If they did, they must have just missed it with their equipment. It was a stroke of bad luck that they didn't hook it.

Jerome and John plunged into the water and did an equipment and buddy safety check before leaving the surface. They were excited to be back in the water and heading to the car. Dan Messaros and I followed Jerome and John by about 5 minutes. I too was very excited to be diving after having missed the previous days dives. I needed to control my emotions and keep my adrenaline in check. I didn't want to have an anxiety attack in 170 feet of water. What new mystery awaited us just below our fins?

Before Dan and I left the surface, we both completed our gear and buddy check. At this point, we were a solid, trusting team. Because the water was so clear, we could easily check the status of our staged tanks suspended below the dive boat on a fixed line to be sure they were hanging in the right spot. From the surface, we could see the stage tanks at 30 and 60 feet. We could also see the tiny bubbles from Jerome and John who were about 150 feet below us. They must have made good time getting to the car. As Dan and I slipped below the surface, I stared down into the black water below, unable to see the bottom.

On the January 13th dive to 150 feet where Dan and I split up for a few minutes and swam in opposite directions, Dan must have been very close to the Warren car. As we descended, I thought about the story he told me regarding a square shaped object he had seen off in the distance before running out of time and turning around. He must have seen the car but not enough of it in the dim light to say for sure it was an old car.

Knowing that the lake bottom was below us was comforting, but scary. As Dan and were descending, it occurred to me that this must be what sky diving was like (something I would discover a few months after I retired), free falling without a tether, totally free. As I began to settle into the shadowy gloom, I had to remind myself to clear my ears (equalize ear pressure) at the surface and often all the way to the car. The cold water and nervousness could make clearing my ears more difficult. I also had to remember to take full deep breaths and to exhale slowly and fully. Our plan was to follow the fixed line down to the car, which gave us a certain amount of security. As we passed the 120-foot-depth level, we could see John and Jerome near the bottom close to a square-shaped object. So far, no issues. At 130 feet, the 1927 Chevy sedan just 30 to 40 feet below us became clearly visible.

On three other occasions we had come extremely close to discovering the car wreck. I remembered the dives that Dan and I had done in December, on January 13 and again on March 24th. As we neared the 1927 Chevy, it occurred to me that if Dan and I had swam east, rather then west on our last dive, we would have run right into it.

At 150 feet, I looked over at Dan Messaros and signaled to him to level off. We had arrived feeling great and were just about 15 feet above the Warren's 1927 Chevy sedan. We needed to hover for a minute to get the digital video camera that Jerome had carried down. Seeing the car for the first time was stunning to say the least. It felt as if there was someone else down here with me aside from the other divers. Could it be the Warrens welcoming us to their final resting place? Maybe Sheriff Pike was cheering us on from far above. I wonder what he would have said about this incredible sight.

I needed to gather my thoughts and get to business. At 150 feet, nitrogen narcosis was beginning to affect me. My peripheral vision was narrowed, and my mind had a numb feeling. This was certainly not our first dive to this depth and certainly not the first time I had felt the effects of nitrogen narcosis. Jacque Cousteau called it the 'rapture of the deep'. We knew this would occur, and we had planned for it. We kept the tasks simple in order to avoid complicated mistakes. We practiced tasks on land before attempting them in the water. We had trained well for this day. Diving to 170 feet with single tanks and large pony tanks sounds crazy and many dive instructors would be highly critical of our dive team. But we built lots of safety into the dive plan to mitigate the risks. Nonetheless, there was a better way to perform this dive, and that would have been with mixed gases and high-capacity double tanks. I would not recommend that recreational divers attempt to dive below 130 feet without proper training and a considerable amount of experience.

Jerome handed me the video camera and shrugged his shoulders, indicating to me that he was not sure if it was working. I hoisted the camera up and turned it on. I dropped to 165 feet and pushed the record button. I began filming as much of the wreck with the divers swimming around as I could, considering the short time we were allowed to visit the wreck. With a minute or two to spare in our eight minutes of bottom time, we headed for the surface. We needed to be conservative on this first dive to the car. Jerome and John stayed at the site for a few more minutes. They would have to make decompression stops on the way back to the surface. We passed two Nitrox 36 tanks with regulators at 90 feet, two more cylinders at 60 feet and then two more at 15 feet. We stopped at the 15 foot marker spent 5 minutes breathing the Nitrox 36 mix. While hanging at 15 feet, I checked my console dive computer and saw that the graph to the far left on the computer screen showed we were still in the green zone with regard to the amount of nitrogen we had absorbed into our tissues. We still had enough air in our single tank and large pony cylinder to easily finish the dive and make an extended safety stop. The Nitrox was refreshing and made both of us feel great after feeling the deep effects of nitrogen narcosis at 165 feet.

When we finally broke he surface, near the dive boat, I shouted to Dr. Paul Gleeson and Barb Maynes "It's the Warren car. The thing is really there. It's unbelievable!." Dan and I climbed aboard the dive boat and removed our cumbersome dive gear. I was anxious to see what the video looked like and to show our surface-support people what we had seen. I opened the video camera housing and played the video tape back to see what we had recorded. I was deeply disappointed to see that the video was out of focus and dark. The news media were standing by waiting for some spectacular video, and we couldn't use it. I examined the setting on the camera and noticed that the automatic focus button had been accidently switched to the off position. It was such a small thing. With the media, timing is everything, and we had just missed the perfect time to make a strong impression. Maybe that's just the way it was supposed to be.

April 13th and 14th were memorable days for the dive team and support staff. We had conducted two dive operations without incident, and we found the car. In fact we had conducted nearly 70 dives on the whole project and had not had one single accident or incident. However, we still had not found Blanche and Russell Warren. Where were they?

On Saturday, May 9, Dan and I returned to the wreck and took several clear 35-mm still photos and digital video of the car. We kept the dive short and within the no-decompression-limit. We used staging tanks and followed the same dive plan as before. The previous dives had proved that our dive planning was solid and thorough. However, we knew there was a better way and our dive planning method would eventually have to change. Bounce diving to the wreck site would have to be replaced with a different type of diving with more safety built into it. That meant we'd need to take additional training in *Extended Range* and *Trimix* diving to effectively and safely dive the site. The new training would allow us to spend more time at the site and conduct an effective search for Blanche and Russell.

The video we took was made exclusively for the Warren family. I was able to copy it to a VHS video tape and personally deliver it to the

Warrens on Whidbey Island the next evening. This time, the underwater digital video camera was set on automatic focus, and the water was crystal clear. The video came out as clear as the water and was stunning, even to an amateur photographer like me. The Warrens were impressed.

Left to right, Geneil Warren, Jerome Ryan, John Rawlings, Dan Messaros, Kristine and Nicholas Warren Grube, Dan Pontbriand, Joe Walker, Bill Walker and Bob Caso.   Courtesy of Olympic National Park

The author, Dan Pontbriand, is exiting the water with technical dive gear at the Warren site on Lake Crescent. Note the double tanks, dry suit, and redundant regulators. This day in mid-August 2003, was unusually calm, clear and warm. Courtesy of Ranger Art Sandison.

11

A GIFT FROM THE DEEP

Up to this point, we had not found any evidence of the Warrens. In mid-May the dive team met to discuss the possible areas that human remains could be found in or around the car. We had conducted several dives searching for more clues. Close examination of the video and 35-mm photos taken by Dan of the surrounding area and the interior of the car failed to show any clear evidence of the Warrens. Photos and videos were important to document the site just as we had found it before anything was touched, disturbed, moved or removed.

Where were the Warrens? Did they die while in the car? Were they thrown out of the car either through the roof or through the windshield as the car turned over? Did they get pinned to the dashboard as the washing machine slid forward, sustaining life-ending injuries?

We consulted with Dr. Paul Gleeson, the Park Cultural Resource Division Chief and asked him what he thought of us conducting a search of the interior of the car for evidence. We wanted to be sure that there were no conflicts since the car was over 50 years old and considered, by law, a Park cultural resource. Dr. Gleeson was very supportive of the idea. He told us the methods used in processing a crime scene were similar to what an archeologist would use to collect evidence at an archeological dig. We were very familiar with collecting crime scene evidence and evidence preservation. We all decided this was a good approach and any evidence would be treated as if it were evidence collected from a crime scene.

We spoke to Rollie, Geneil and Kristine Warren about the removal of items from the interior of the car. Rollie agreed that the best chance of finding his grandparents would be to search the interior and the area immediately around the outside of the car. Searching under the car

144

was going to be a problem since moving the car was not going to be practical. We also talked to Bob Caso and advised him of our plans.

John Rawlings and Jerome Ryan reminded us of an object inside the car they had seen on the very first dive to the wreck. It was an object that appeared to have pleats as if it were folded or perhaps made in that fashion. We searched the photos and videos and found the object that John and Jerome had seen. It looked like a purse or a bag or a piece of clothing.

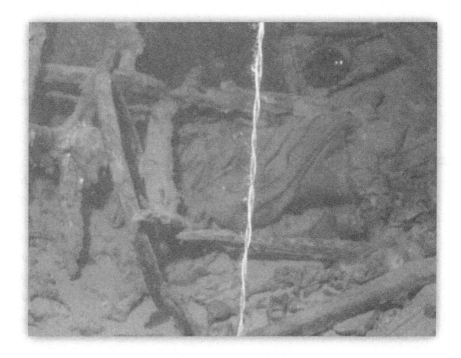

At the center of the photo is the object the dive team focused on removing and examining. It looked like a cloth object with pleats and appeared to be folded. Note the round steering wheel at left center, the frame of the seat surrounding the cloth object and the bottom of a glass beverage bottle near the top of the photo. The wire in the center of the photo is from the dome light. Courtesy of Olympic National Park.

Dan Messaros and I decided to conduct a short bounce dive to the site on May 23 to further document the contents of the car with emphasis on the unknown object behind the steering wheel and to continue our search for human remains. We videotaped the object of special interest. I saw Dan reach out and touch it after having photographed it. It looked like a bolt of cloth, possibly a piece of clothing or a bag of some type. Could this be Blanche's handbag or maybe a small shopping bag?

We planned to dive the site on Saturday, June 2nd, assisted by Jerome Ryan and John Rawlings. Bob Caso, Bill Walker and the Warren family were there to support the dive operation, hoping that we would find Blanche and Russell. We anchored our boat near the now-familiar Pelican Buoy floating about six feet below the surface in the clear waters of the Lake. Dan and I splashed at about 11:00 a.m., with Bill Walker handling surface-support Divemaster duties and Bob Caso assisting. Dan and I carried with us several nylon mesh dive bags and a five-gallon plastic bucket with lid to secure the cloth-like object.

The aqua blue water was cold but clear. As we slipped beneath the surface and began our descent following the nylon yellow line into the abyss the color of the water turned a dark greyish-green as we passed 100 feet. Water as it gets deeper, filters out the various spectrums of light. As Dan and I descended, we could see the edge of the cliff to our south about 60 feet away. As we passed 120 feet, we could make out the base of the wall below us at 160 feet deep. We turned on our flashlights and began looking for the car. At about 130 feet, following the yellow line attached to the car, we began to see the outline of the car, its form clear and unmistakable. Approaching it we were both very conscious of our fins and the amount of silt they would kick up. We wanted good visibility inside the car. Some four minutes has passed since we left the surface. Dan and I approached the interior of the car and made ready our bucket and dive bags. We slowly maneuvered ourselves so that we were now headfirst inside the car. I reached out with my dive gloves and slipped them under the cloth object. I wanted to be careful to not move too fast in hopes of avoiding as much silt and cloudy visibility as possible. I gently lifted the object and placed it into the bucket that Dan had perfectly positioned next to me. We had practiced this technique on land before attempting it in 170 feet of water. The lift created a big cloud of silt, which was apparently unavoidable. Our task now complete, we headed for the surface.

Our time on the bottom was about five minutes, several minutes ahead of schedule and well within the no-decompression limit. John and Jerome, having splashed just after we had, dropped below the car and descended to 200 feet, hoping to find the remains of Blanche and Russell. Dan and I surfaced without incident. Jerome and John completed their decompression stops and surfaced fifty minutes later and unfortunately did not see any additional evidence.

On top, eager hands were awaiting the cache of goods from the depths of the lake. Having motored back to the dive locker, we carried our evidence into the building. Bob Caso was most anxious to see what we had found, as was I. We donned latex gloves and found a plastic wash basin to clean whatever it was we were about to examine. We asked Kristine Warren, the daughter of Rollie Warren and great-grand daughter of Blanche Warren, to assist us. What we had just removed from the lake was likely owned by Blanche. So it seemed only fitting that Kristine should help us. Her skills as a dental assistant would come in handy.

We removed the object from the pail and laid it out on a plastic sheet. It became clear almost immediately the object was a nylon or rayon fabric with pleats, buttons, sleeves, and stitching. At first we thought it was a dress. Safety pins were inserted in some of the seams, indicating the piece was a work in progress. It became clear that Blanche had been making herself a jacket. Attached to the jacket was a heavy, rusty crank handle used to start the car engine, a very rusty pair of pliers, a screwdriver and a small grease gun. These tools were so badly rusted that they were almost unrecognizable. The rust was so thick that the tools stuck to the blouse as if they had been glued. The blouse was probably folded with the scissors and pins tucked inside and fell onto the tools as the car plunged forward in its course toward the bottom of the lake. The crushed passenger and driver seats smashed down on the blouse further compressing it into the tools

The most stunning object we found on the blouse was a small piece of jewelry in the form of a silver art-deco snake pin. The pin was about three inches long and had thirteen small gemstones that looked like diamonds, one of which was missing. In its place was a small piece of tin foil or similar foil. Kristine was deeply moved by the sight of the delicate pin. It had belonged to her great-grandmother and was last seen and by touched by her 72 years ago. The small piece of silver foil in one of the jewel holes suggested the pin was valuable to Blanche and reflected her modesty. I was stunned.

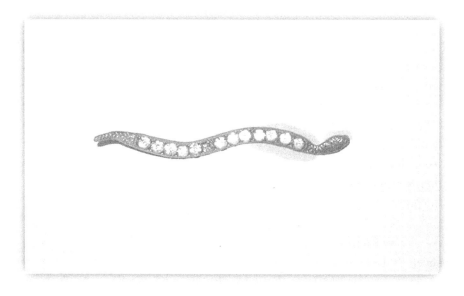

The silver pin shortly after it was removed from the blouse that Blanche was sewing. Note that there are 12 jewels in place with one missing. A small piece of shiny tin foil (not shown) was in place of the missing jewel. Courtesy of Olympic National Park.

Stuck to the blouse along with the pin were several small objects that looked like small harpoons. The objects appeared to be made of bone with a black stringy substance attached. The stringy substance seemed similar to hair. We removed the suspected hair sample from the blouse. I secured it in a small jar filled with Lake Crescent water, the same water it had been in for the past 72 years. We also found a hard, dense object that appeared to be a tooth, perhaps a molar. It was stuck to the cloth thanks to the nearby rusty tools. It was enamel white in color. It could have been non-organic (a rock), but it was very difficult to tell without a microscope. We videotaped the examination of the blouse just in case the materials we had removed were human remains. Each object was photographed, preserved in an evidence container, and recorded on an evidence log.

Common sense suggested that if human remains were attached to the blouse, they must be from Blanche Warren. Forensic analysis would be needed to determine if the evidence was an organic substance. If they were human in origin, would they contain DNA?

The next day, June 3, the Warren family remained in Port Angeles. That evening, team members were invited to dinner at a local restaurant in Port Angeles by the Warren family. Geneil Warren told me that she would be having a little celebration for Kristine, her daughter, to celebrate her 33rd birthday.

Dan Messaros and I decided to give Kristine the silver pin as a birthday gift, since the pin had little evidentiary value to the case, but would be a priceless family heirloom, considering where it was found. I found a Mason canning jar and filled it with Lake Crescent water, then placed the silver snake pin in it, sealing it with a tin lid. I placed a red ribbon around the jar and lid and found a birthday card that the team members signed. That evening, we gave the gift to Kristine. In essence, this was really a gift from her great-grandmother from the depths of the lake. The team was just the conduit for delivering it.

Kristine's great-grandmother would have been 35 years old when she died, just a few years older than Kristine. Their physical similarities were striking. The Warren family genes were prominent.

A few days later, I called the local FBI office in Silverdale, Washington, and talked to a Special Agent. I explained the details of the case and of our desire to have the material examined forensically. During the second week of June, I delivered the evidence to the Special Agent who would see that it was processed. Rollie also expressed a strong desire to know if the evidence contained the remains of his grandmother, Blanche Warren.

On June 16, at about 7:30 p.m. Kristine Warren (Grube) and I arrived at Madrona Point with the ashes of Frank Warren, the eldest son of Blanche and Russell Warren. Frank died in 1972 in Enumclaw, Washington, and was cremated. His son, James Warren, was in possession of his remains and submitted a request to Olympic National Park for a Special Permit to have his ashes placed near his parents at Lake Crescent. His ashes had been held for 30 years awaiting the proper moment to lay them to rest.

On this evening, the air temperature was about 55 degrees. Thick clouds were scattered to the east and west of Madrona Point threatening rain. There was no wind. With Kristine supervising, I took Frank Warren's ashes and spread them on rocks and grasses on the lake shore about 100 feet east of the Ambulance Point near the *"little curve in the highway"* and a few feet from the exact spot where the Warren car left the road. Then I returned to the beach in the small cove where Kristine was standing. We looked to the east at the final resting place of the Warren car and then looked to the shore where we had placed the ashes. We returned a son to his parents after a separation of nearly 73 years.

We looked to the east, we saw a family of Merganser ducks with a brood of nine ducklings overhead. They landed on the water near the resting place of the Warren car. After two minutes the ducks swam directly over the car. It began to rain lightly and the winds picked up. The ashes that had been placed on the shore slowly washed into the lake. The sky above opened up and shafts of light filtered down to the lake. It was a magical moment. Frank was truly in the arms of his loving parents

In late June, the FBI called the Storm King Ranger Station and told us the suspected tooth was a small rock and non-organic. What we hoped might be human hair was thread from the blouse and was composed of rayon, a common clothing material in 1929. The whereabouts of Blanche and Russell Warren were still a mystery.

By early July of 2002, no clear evidence of Blanche and Russell had been found in or around the Chevy sedan. The dive team needed to discuss the future of the investigation. The diving, thus far, had gone without any incidents or accidents, but we needed to be sure that the potential results were commensurate with the risks we were taking. With what we knew, was it worth it to continue to search for the remains of Blanche and Russell Warren?

12

RETURN

In July, the dive team met at the Barnes Point dive locker and covered a number of compelling questions.

First, was Blanche with Russell at the time of the accident on the evening of July 3rd ? Russell reportedly picked up his wife at the Lincoln Hospital at about 3:30 p.m. and carried two suitcases out of the hospital, suggesting that Blanche may have been in the hospital for an extended amount of time. According to Blanche's Lincoln Hospital roommate, Mrs. K. E. Rudolph, as Russell and Blanche left the hospital, Blanche *"declared that she wanted to go home for the Fourth of July with her two sons and both she and Warren seemed happy over the prospect."* What she was being treated for, we do not know. However, back in 1929 and even today, small hospitals tended to put patients who had surgery together as roommates. Since Mrs. K. E. Rudolph had surgery, it is possible that Blanche also had surgery.

A Port Angeles Evening News story dated August 10, reported that Cliff Wilson, a friend of Russell's, who talked to him the night before he came to Port Angeles, stated *"on a previous visit into the hospital he fell asleep at the wheel when going around Lake Crescent, and when he woke up was cross-wise (sic) in the road, heading for the lake."* Wilson also said that Russell , *"stopped his auto, went down to the lake and bathed his hands and face before proceeding on that trip"*. This provides further evidence that Blanche may have had some type of surgery that required an extended recovery since Russell apparently had made more than one trip to the hospital

Wilson declared that, " *They certainly were planning to come back, because the last thing Warren said to me was that he had to be back to Bogachiel by July Fourth because he promised the kids they would spend the day at the Sol Duc Hot Springs. He also promised Joe Lyondecker (sic) to start on the pulp wood work again on July Fifth or Sixth as the work was behind".*

Secondly, did Russell fall asleep at the wheel while traveling to Port Angeles on morning of July 3? There is no statement from anyone saying that he did. But he had apparently been working very hard and long hours to fill his pulp wood contract with Joe Leyendecker. Apparently Russell made more than one trip to Port Angeles to visit his wife and Wilson did state Russell fell asleep at the wheel on a previous trip.

Next, what evidence was there to support the theory that Russell may have fallen asleep again while traveling back to Quillayute Prairie on the evening of July 3 after he picked up Blanche? There was evidence to support the idea that the car may have been traveling slowly, possibly as slow as 10 miles per hour, suggesting that Russell may have again fallen asleep at the wheel. Had he been traveling faster, say 25 or 30 miles per hour and then was driven off the road by a passing log truck, there would have been more vehicle damage, especially to the front end. The only damage visible to the divers was a dent on the left wheel. That damage could have happened when the car exited the roadway and struck the cedar tree, or it could have happened by hitting a large rock in the roadway, resulting in loss of control of the car. What we do know about drivers who fall asleep at the wheel while the vehicle is in motion is they release pressure from the gas pedal slowing the vehicle down. We also know from experience that vehicles slowly drift in one direction, either to the left, over the center of the roadway, or to the right side of the road, leaving no yaw or skid marks..

The 1927 Chevy sedan the Warrens owned was used when they bought it and barely two years old. The previous owner was known to Sheriff Pike. The car was likely in good mechanical condition, considering that it had less than 2,000 thousand miles on it. In 2007, I visited the Warren car and examined the odometer which read 1,967 miles. Cars in the 1920s were drafty and had less than airtight wooden floorboards. Could it be that the passenger compartment was filled with carbon monoxide from a leaking muffler? The windows may have been rolled up to keep dust out from other cars. Maybe Russell passed out and succumbed to carbon monoxide poisoning, rather than falling asleep.

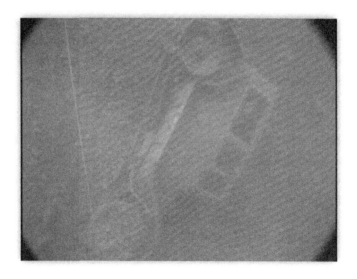

The Warren car in 171 feet of water. Note the two wheels. The front tire and wheel turned hauntingly free when divers accidently brushed up against it. It appears to be undamaged. The rear wheel is slightly dented and the tire is flat which could have happened on July 3, 1929 when it struck a cedar tree laying near the shore. Courtesy of Olympic National Park.

Did Blanche and Russell Warren leave the Lincoln Hospital and drive without stopping toward Quillayute Prairie? Could it be that Blanche and Russell stopped at the Singer Tavern for a drink, perhaps an early Fourth of July beverage or drink? They would have passed right by the Singer Tavern on the way home.

Although 1929 was during the Prohibition (sale and possession of alcoholic beverage was prohibited by law), many establishments were known to serve a drink or two in backrooms and basements. It was rather easy to find a drink. It would have taken them about 15 to 20 minutes at 20 to 30 miles per hour to reach Laird's Corner from the Lincoln Hospital, a distance of about 6 or 7 miles and west of Port Angeles on the Olympic Highway. They would have passed Laird's Corner at about 3:45 or 3:50 P.M. This place was the last sighting of Blanche and Russell as they headed west. Like the Singer Tavern, this was a place that could have sold beverages to the Warrens. Small brown beverage bottles were found inside the Warren car. However, Russell was not known to be a drinker of alcoholic beverages. Perhaps the bottles were from soda pop.

The drive to Lake Crescent is about another 12 miles or 25 to 30 minutes of driving time at 25 to 30 miles per hour. This would place them on the east end of Lake Crescent at about 4:15 p.m. to 4:20 p.m. No confirmed and creditable reports from witnesses came forth in 1929 stating the Warrens stopped anywhere along the route toward home.

If the Warrens had continued to drive west on the Olympic Highway without stopping, they would have arrived at Madrona Point at about 4:30 p.m. or 4:45 p.m., which would have been the approximate time of the accident. Blanche and Russell's own statements suggested they were in a hurry to get home to be with their boys. If they did stop, it would have been only for a few minutes to get fuel for the car, the bathroom or something to drink to subdue a parched throat.

In July 2002, the dive team and Rangers were tied up with the Park's routine seasonal operations and training. We managed to fit in one dive at the car site in mid-July to search other areas in shallower waters. The Warrens had to be in or near their car somewhere.

One thing we all noticed as we probed the car and examined pictures and video, was it appeared to be relatively undamaged. The front end was undamaged. The front bumper did not display evidence of impact or damage; neither did the radiator, front grill engine cover, front passenger-side fender or the headlight. Although the headlamp appeared to have an imploded lens cover, that could have been due to the water pressure.

The two wheel assemblies were visible on the passenger side. Only the rear one seemed to have some damage. The front tire exhibited what looked like full tire pressure. The tread was in good shape, and the sidewall appeared to be undamaged, suggesting this tire was not flat when the car went into the water. It's likely the tire is full of water rather than air, which is why it appeared to be perfectly round without defect. If it was full of air, water pressure at 150 feet would have deflated it as you see. When divers accidently touched the wheel, it was free and loose allowing it to spin hauntingly even after, now 73 (as of July 3, 2002) years of being underwater!

The rear tire appeared to be flat or deflated. This could have happened due to the depth of the water and pressure. This does not rule out the idea that the car could have sustained a flat tire while driving west and coming around Madrona Point, which could have caused Russell Warren to lose control of the car near the road edge as the car went around the *"little curve in the highway."*

The passenger side of the car appeared to be undamaged. The running board, rear bumper, spare-tire assembly, and taillight all appeared to be undamaged.

The front passenger-side headlight lens looks imploded, probably due to water pressure. The light, otherwise, appears to be undamaged as does the rest of the car that is visible. Courtesy of Olympic National Park.

The Warren car lying on its side in 171 feet of water. Notice the large dent on the top of the windshield frame (left arrow). The dent was probably caused by the vehicle turning upside-down striking the cedar tree that was laying on the shore and in the water. The car's dome light can be seen hanging by an electrical wire (up arrow). Courtesy of Olympic National Park.

Nearly all the windows in the car were broken, damaged, or missing. Given the amount of rock fall in the area, the fact that the car's resting place is on a 45 degree slope and the large amount of road construction over the last 73 years, broken windows are to be expected. The broken windows could have caused the fish Bill Walker saw to have the scars and scratches on their sides.

There were two sections of the car that were clearly damaged. It was likely created when the car fell off the road and began its plunge into the depths of the lake. The windshield frame had a significant dent and the roof was entirely missing. The windshield frame was probably damaged when it hit a tree as the vehicle turned over just as it left the road. This would have broken out the windshield glass, scattering it all over the lake bottom just the way Sheriff Pike found it in August of 1929. The roof was missing and likely torn off by the same cedar tree with help from the impact of the washing machine.

The steering wheel was found near the steering wheel post without any of the support arms needed to attach it to the post. It could be the support arms just rusted away, or it could be the driver impacted the steering wheel with his chest, breaking the wheel. It could also be the washing machine hit the wheel and broke it. There just isn't enough evidence to support any of the possible scenarios. What was becoming apparent was there were no large bones inside the car. Even after 73 years, the bones, if bones were there inside the car, they should be recognizable as they would have had some protected from the crushing and grinding of falling rock from above.

But there weren't any sizeable bones. Large bones like femurs, lower leg bones, upper extremity bones and vertebra should have survived. What is the chemistry of the water in Lake Crescent and would it de-calcify bones? As it turns out, the Park Water Treatment Lab stationed at Lake Crescent had completed a recent analysis of the water and Lake Crescent is relatively low in calcium of which bones are mostly made of. Perhaps the bones may have just turned to chalk and disappeared.

The washing machine that Russell bought while in Port Angeles wasn't in the car, nor was it anywhere near the car. In fact, we never found any part of it with the exception of the lid. The rest of the washing machine had to be somewhere below the car. With it being round, it could have tumbled all the way down to the next shelf about 350 feet deep.

Could Russell and Blanche have descended into the inky depths of the lake to that same depth? One of the things we noticed was there didn't appear to be a large number of obstacles below two hundred feet. The bottom continued to drop at a constant slope of about 35 to 45 degrees all the way to 325 feet to a shelf. The width of the shelf is perhaps 100 feet wide and then it drops off again at a sharp angle to a depth of 624 feet, the deepest part of the lake. At 325 feet the shelf is large enough to catch and stop any object that might roll down the slope from above. Could the washing machine and the both Warrens be at that depth? The challenge of searching the lake bottom at that depth would be daunting.

Luckily, we had a few friends who showed a strong interest in Lake Crescent and the Warren case. Dale and Ed Jacobs, a father-and-son team of underwater explorers from Oregon had been coming here for several months, even before this phase of the Warren case began. Their hobby was to design and build a functioning ROV to explore lakes and ocean. In July of 2002, the Jacobs came to Lake Crescent to test their newly built ROV, named Janet. They enjoyed the Lake's clear, clean water conducting sea trials with the ROV. The clear water made it easy to see and control it. Use of ROV's to this point were not regulated by the National Park Service. The new rules would not take effect until 2005.

Dan Messaros and I met with the Jacobs on a late July weekend day while they were running their boat.. We asked if they'd be interested in experimenting with their ROV at the Warren site and if so would they be interesting in searching the area below the Warren car. They gladly agreed and seemed to be excited to be a part of the case. Although I couldn't offer them compensation or even ask them to be VIP's (official volunteers), they were excited to give the idea a try. They were also well aware of the Warren case from Internet articles and TV and newspaper stories.

Over the next few weeks, we saw the Jacobs several times working the ROV at the Warren site. Dan Messaros and I watched carefully as the Jacobs applied their skills and experimented with their new toy. They videotaped their search efforts and provided the videos to our dive team for examination. The Jacobs reported that they did not find any additional clues while searching the depths of the lake below the wreck all the way down to 325 feet. They did find a few pieces of scrap metal and an iron cog from a machine that could have come from the Warren car. The cog was about 12 inches in diameter and 3 inches across and made of heavy iron. The cog had been seen by other divers diving the Warren car and was about 180 feet deep, slightly west of the Warren car.

On July 4, 2002, three generations of the Warren family, gathered at Lake Crescent to memorialize Blanche and Russell. Many had never met each other. At about 2:00 p.m., the family traveled to Madrona Point and gathered at the shoreline overlooking the final resting place of Blanche and Russell Warren and their son, Frank. The missing couple had never been declared dead and death certificates were never issued. The service was to finally put closure to the Warren mystery.

A priest from Port Angeles presided and a bagpipe player played. In the words of Rollie Warren, "*It was a very emotional moment for everybody. I saw tears in a lot of people's eye, mine included.*" James Warren, the son of Frank Warren, gave the eulogy. It was a fitting end to the Warren mystery and to a remarkable journey for the Warren family. As the year 2002 came to a close, Blanche and Russell still had not been found. The team continued to dive with far less frequency, staying above 130 feet in depth. No new evidence was found, but local and regional interest in the case remained high. Divers from Seattle-Tacoma, Portland, and other cities were coming to dive the now-famous site. However, the Warren investigation was not over yet.

In 2003, I completed IANTD Extended Range and Trimix scuba training with Jerome Ryan as my instructor. I also completed a cave diving course in Florida. Bill Walker and his son, Joe completed the same training. We were now trained to dive with double tanks, staging tanks, and Trimix gas qualifying us to go beyond 130 feet and to stay longer. These extended dives would require decompression stops on the way to the surface, just as John Rawlings and Jerome Ryan had been doing. The new training was beyond the Olympic National Park dive program. I need to get permission from the National Park Service Dive Control Board if I was going to dive below 130 feet with Trimix. I would also need to have an National Park Service dive partner that was trained to dive to those depths which meant that any future decompression dives and extended range dives were going to be on my own time outside the National Park Service dive program.

Interestingly, the National Park Service Pacific West Regional Dive Officer issued me a dive certification card with a depth rating of 190 feet. I was limited to using compressed air and Nitrox in my tanks rather than the Trimix I had recently been trained to use.

In 2003, the Olympic National Park top management was replaced by an all new t eam. A new Superintendent, Assistant Superintendent, and Chief Ranger, and, a bit later, Assistant Chief Ranger were hired. The new management group was not familiar with the case and approached the issue with a great deal of caution. I am sure if I had been in their shoes, I would have looked at this case with a great deal of skepticism, considering the risks that the dive team was taking, risks that non-divers would have considered too extreme. However, we still had strong support from the Regional Dive Officer and many of the park employees.

The management team's skepticism was understandable. We needed to convince them we understood the level of risk and were mitigating each concern with training and a high level of planning. I am sure there were a few employees who thought the park dive team was reaching too far and that someone was going to get injured or die. I was doing everything in my power to see that our team was doing everything possible to conduct safe dives. Someday, our divers or other divers would find something, I was sure of it.

Rollie and Geneil Warren and their daughter Kristine, all agreed however it was time to put the case to rest and. With that being said, we needed to return some of the artifacts we had removed from the car. Nearly all of the clues and evidence we had collected relating to the missing couple had were turned over to the Warrens or were in the possession of the Clallam County Historical Society. The County Museum wanted to create a display the artifacts.

During the spring of 2004, a team of volunteer divers from the Seattle area met and agreed to return the blouse and several of the other artifacts to the Warren car. The names of the divers were, by now very familiar to the Park Dive Team and the Warren family. John Rawlings, Jerome Ryan, Randy Williams, Dan Warter, Carl Stieglitz, Phil Breed, Greg Gambill and Bill Walker, were all technical divers trained with rebreathers and double tanks.

On Saturday, May 29th , 2004, the divers all lined up on the shoreline at Ambulance Point (Madrona Point) on the small beach and cove that faced the east. From the beach, the divers staged their entry into the water. It was a short 250 foot surface swim to the *"little curve in the highway."* Forty feet below the surface, the divers could see the hole or ancient water fall. All the divers had to do was follow the waterfall slide that extended down to the edge of the cliff at about 100 feet, drop over the edge and follow the wall down to a depth of 160 feet. The Warren car was just a short distance from the bottom of the wall. Before leaving the surface, Randy Williams took possession of the blouse from Kristine Warren Grube and packed it into the now-empty urn that had once contained the remains of Frank Warren. Randy would place the urn with the blouse inside, next to the car at 170 feet.

I was on shore and not diving since it was a work day for me. I was on lake patrol, however, and had beached the Park dive patrol boat on the beach at Ambulance (Madrona) Point just as the divers were preparing their gear. The divers departed the beach area and began the swim toward the dive site as the Warren family (Kristine, Rollie, Geneil and little Nicholas), all waved, wishing them a safe dive. The divers all descended together. Some of the divers were assigned search patterns east, west, and a bit deeper than the Warren car, but all were to scrutinize the area in close proximity to the car.

The photo was taken on Saturday, May 29, 2004 at the small beach located at Ambulance (Madrona) Point. Phil Gambill, is getting his gear ready for a technical dive to the Warren car. Courtesy of Olympic National Park.

The Warren family and I stood on shore and watched bubbles surface from the divers now 170 to 200 feet deep. I had been involved in many dives at this site and so far, there had been no injured divers and no serious incidents. We were either lucky or good at what we were doing. I think it was both.

About 75 minutes later, divers began to surface. First, one diver, then two, three, four, five, six and then number seven. *Where was diver number eight?* Were we missing someone? The Divemaster was Randy Williams. He accounted for all the divers on the surface ensuring they returned safely except John Rawlings. Where was John?

Suddenly, one of the divers said he could hear a voice down shore toward the east. I was standing on the beach searching the surface of the water with my eyes and looked toward the east at the shoreline. I saw what appeared to be John sitting on a rock near the shore in shallow water. Fearing he was injured or needed assistance, I launched the dive patrol boat and motored over to John's position. Randy Williams was on board in case John needed in-water assistance. I asked him if he was OK. His mask and hood were off, but he was still wearing the rest of his dive gear. I looked at his face, and it looked like he had seen a ghost.. John said, *"I'm OK, but I found Russell Warren."* At first I thought he was joking. I said, *"You found Russell? Where?"* He pointed to the area of the lake directly in front of us.

While ascending and conducting his first decompression stop at 150 feet, he paused at a large tree root wad lying on its side using it to balance himself for the required time. As he looked down at the bottom, he saw a white, round object about the size of a softball. As he approached the object it began to look like a skull. He touched the object and felt that it was very brittle. It was a human skull. Next to it was what appeared to be a femur, a human femur. The femur appeared to be about the same size in length as his own. John stands about 6 feet 2 inches tall, a bit taller than Russell Warren. John boarded the dive patrol boat and we transported him back to the beach area to the waiting divers and the Warren family. As I jumped off the boat and secured the line, it required

165

all of my strength not to rush up to the Warrens and tell them the news. That was now John's job. I gathered everyone together on the beach and announced that John had some incredible news.

John began by saying, *"I think I found Russell Warren."* He then went on to tell the rest of the story to the group. Geneil Warren was stunned and so was Kristine. I noticed large tears in my eyes. There were some stunned faces amongst the divers too!

13

RECOVERY

A new dive plan had to be formulated to confirm the location of the human remains. I had seen a number of human remains including skeletons and skulls, but these were all on land. These bones were 150 feet below the surface. How was I going to secure the location and preserve it as evidence? First, I needed to see the bones. As a law enforcement Ranger, I still needed to confirm they were human and not an animal even though I knew John was probably correct. I knew that diving below 130 feet would raise a lot of negative feeling at Park Headquarters. I also suspected that the Chief Ranger would object to any dive at the site by a Park Service Diver. I decided to wait until after I was off duty to conduct the dive. I asked Randy Williams, Bill Walker, and Dan Warter, who had a video camera, to make the dive with me.

I called Olympics' dispatch office to provide them with a verbal report of the incident and found the Acting Chief Ranger was the Park's Criminal Investigator, Glen Melville. He had been working as a Criminal Investigator for a little over a year and was new to the Park Service. I gave him a full report. He said he would be coming out to Lake Crescent and would arrive in about an hour. Before we hung up the phone, I asked him for permission to dive the site to confirm the bones were human. He stated, yes.

At about 4:00 p.m., Acting Chief Ranger Glen Melville and Ranger Aaron Titus arrived by boat. I asked Glen if he was OK with me making the dive. He again said I should go ahead with the dive to locate the bones. My dive partners were Randy Williams, Bill Walker, and Dan Warter. Our two jobs were to string a line from the shoreline to the location of the bones so that we could easily find the site in the future and to capture some video to help confirm the bones were likely human.

After all the difficulties of finding the car, I had learned a lesson. We needed to go back into the water today while memories were still fresh and locate the site. We could not wait days or weeks to form another dive team. The job needed to be done today. We had plenty of gear, plenty of highly qualified divers, and plenty of time to formulate a solid and safe dive plan.

I had never been diving with Randy Williams or Dan Warter. I knew they were both excellent divers and very confident in their skills. At about 5:30 p.m. after I was off duty, the three of us departed the surface with a video camera and a lot of line to string from the surface to the bones. As we descended, we followed the waterfall slide as if going to the car site. When we arrived at the bottom of the waterfall, we dropped over the edge and began swimming in an easterly direction angling down along the wall. As we passed 130 feet, stringing line behind us, a large tree root wad came into view about 20 feet below. John Rawlings had said the bones were a few feet to the west of the root wad. As we approached the root wad, Bill and I looked down and clearly saw what John had seen. Amazing! Absolutely amazing! Dan Warter had seen the same thing at the same time and began to record the bones with his digital video camera. Randy attached the line to the root wad and stayed near the base of the tree while Dan, Bill and I hovered over the bones. The femur rested about one foot from the skull and at the same depth. This was likely the remains of Russell Warren. But was it?

Not surprisingly, the femur was clean of flesh; it looked thick, but fragile. As I waved my glove over the bones, I could see a small cloud of white calcium, suggesting that the bones were very soft. Was this where Russell's body came to rest? Or had his body been resting in shallower water and drifted down to this depth? Two bones of different weight and density next to each other at this depth and suggested that this was where Russell Warren died if the wreck did not kill him outright.. A human skull and femur are rather dense and strong bones. The fact they endured nearly 75 years underwater, surviving rock slides, earthquakes, and the chemistry of the water was a near miracle.

Early in the investigation and with a great deal of optimism, we had consulted with the King County Forensic Anthropologist, asking her what bones would look like after being immersed in water for 72 years. She stated that it all depends on the chemistry and temperature of the water. She told us that bones would likely survive many years underwater if the conditions were right. As previously mentioned, the Park Water Lab Technician tested the lake water and found it was calcium deficient. The tests led us to believe that bones might dissolve in the lake after an unknown amount of time. To test the theory, I placed a box of animal bones in the lake near Barnes Point in late 2001. By the summer of 2004, the bones appeared to be in the same condition as when I placed them there, .Admittedly, it was only 3 years and not 72 years. Bones just might indeed last a long time in Lake Crescent.

We left the bones in place, not touching or disturbing them. As I elevated 10 feet above them, preparing to begin our ascent to the surface, I looked to the west in the direction of the Warren car and could make out its distinctive shape. We were about 60 feet east of it and 20 feet shallower in depth. Either Russell Warren's body had drifted and settled on the bottom at this location, or the car, with momentum, drifted after throwing him (and probably Blanche) out before it came to rest. Russell's body was just a short distance from his car considering the circumstances of the accident..

If these bones were not Russell, then who were they? Could they be Blanche? Could the skull be Blanche's and the femur Russell's? Although highly unlikely, could the bones be Native American? Maybe they were the remains of an unreported accident or incident?

We surfaced safely and reported back to the beach. Many of the divers had departed, heading to homes in Seattle and the surrounding area. However, the Warrens were there to greet us with warm smiles and plenty of emotional comfort. Acting Chief Ranger Glen Melville was also on shore. We discussed closing the area to prevent contamination, disturbance, and possible theft.

Barb Maynes, the Park Public Information Officer wrote a press release, The story went all over the Pacific Northwest and beyond. The press release was written conservatively saying that bones had been found but the identity of the person had not yet been determined. DNA analysis would be needed.

In the days that followed, plans were developed to recover the bones, utilizing the National Park Service's elite Submerged Resources Center (SRC) dive team, formerly the Submerged Cultural Resource Unit or SCRU. The SRC dive team had a long history of tackling complicated underwater projects such as the Warren case. The SRC was a leader amongst Federal government dive programs since the late 1970s and had a remarkable safety record. This team was clearly what we needed to finish the job. See appendix B for more details on the SRC.

The SRC is well known throughout the world. They have assisted with many important projects such as the recovery of the Civil War-era submarine *HMS Hunley*. SRC surveyed the Bikini Atoll WW-II shipwrecks as well as the *USS Arizona* in Pearl Harbor. They have contributed to many articles in *National Geographic Magazine*, documentaries on the *History* and *Discovery Channels*. They have worked closely with *Woods Hole Institute* (which helped find the *HMS Titanic* with Robert Ballard) and many other educational, commercial and government agencies. We were glad to have them to assist with the Warren mystery.

In September of 2004, the SRC agreed to assist the park's dive team with recovering the bones using state-of-the art scientific and forensic methods. The Warren case was about to receive the highest level of professional service. The incoming team was composed of Brett Seymour, the team's underwater photographer, Dr. Dave Conlin, specializing in marine archaeology, and James Bradford, an archeologist specializing in ancient human remains. These three specialists were also all highly skilled technical divers.

The SRC dive team arrived in the park on November 30. Much needed to be done to get all the gear ready. The dive team would be using a 80 percent helium and 20 percent oxygen mixed gas. This mixture would eliminate nitrogen from the compressed gas we would be breathing and eliminate any nitrogen narcosis. Eight sets of double tanks filled with the special mix were collected from Randy William's Starfish Dive Center in Seattle.

The team also brought a VideoRay ROV. The small, rabbit-sized ROV, would be the perfect tool for searching and surveying around the Warren car and would give the three new divers a good orientation to the site.

On Saturday December 4, 2004, Dave Conlin and Jim Bradford deployed the ROV into the waters of Lake Crescent and navigated it at the bone site. John Rawlings was also on the boat. He was anxious to see what the bones looked like after six months, hoping they were undisturbed. The ROV quickly located the car and then moved up the slope searching for the large root wad and the bones . When the root wad came into view of the ROV's video camera. John Rawlings directed Dr. Conlin, the ROV operator to move the vehicle slightly to the west. The skull and femur came into view and appeared to be in the same condition as they were when discovered six months earlier.

Brett and Dave decided to search for more human remains in the vicinity. More bones must be nearby. Perhaps the remains of Blanche could be found. The ROV did not have the limitations of a human diver and could stay underwater as long as the pilot was at the controls and the generator provided power.

The ROV moved deeper directly below the root wad. Light from the surface grew dimmer. It was equipped with a powerful forward looking light that helped provide light to the attached camera. The ROV approached 200 feet in depth and spotted an unusual looking rock formation that looked like a pyramid about three feet tall. As the vehicle scoured the surrounding terrain, another bone was spotted by the team.

Dr. Conlin carefully and slowly navigated the vehicle toward bone recording the site with the video camera. This one also appeared to be femur, but in much worse condition than the femur found above. This one exhibited a black color on its surface and was thinner. Was this also a femur from Russell Warren? Was it his other leg? The ROV continued to search the area for another hour. The Warren family, at Lake Crescent for the weekend, was told of the second femur. Now we had three bones to retrieve and examine.

On Sunday, December 5, Brett Seymour, Dr. Dave Conlin, Jim Bradford, and I were at the dive locker at Lake Crescent bright and early. This would be one of two days dedicated to the bone-recovery operation. A large number of scuba cylinders and gear needed to be loaded aboard the boats and transported to the dive site. The first day's mission was to dive to car and the two bone sites in addition to introducing the new SRC divers to the sites.

Two decompression stations were hung on rope below the boat using eight-foot long horizontal PVC pipe for each. One deco station was at 20 feet and the other was at 30 feet. Surface supplied scuba regulators on long hoses supplying 100 percent oxygen were attached to the bars at both stations. In addition to the twin 102-cubic-foot cylinders containing the helium and oxygen mix that each diver carried on his back, each diver also carried two 80 cubic foot stage cylinders under each arm with Nitrox 32 and Nitrox 80. The divers carried enough mixed gas to finish the dive in the event of an equipment malfunction. Additionally, each divers also had enough gear and gas to help a dive buddy in the event there was a gear failure. Any such failure would result in aborting the dive.

Dr. Conlin and I splashed first, quickly descending to the car. We rigged a down line to it and leaving a Nitrox bailout tank attached to it at 140 feet. Then we attached a travel line to the car and swam to the bone site at near the root wad. Next we carried the travel line from the bone cache site down to the single femur at 202 feet lashing it to the pyramid shaped rock. Lastly, we swam with the travel line directly back to the car, attaching it to the bumper, forming a rough triangle. We wanted Brett and Jim to easily find the car and the two bone sites. Their mission was to document the sites with cameras and writing slates.

As soon as Dave and I had completed our task, we began our ascent to the surface. At 150 feet, we looked up slope and spotted the bailout tank 10 feet above. This was our cue to switch from our Heliox gas mix (what we had been breathing for the past thirty minutes) to our first staging tank of Nitrox 32 mix. I delayed switching to the mix until I had reached 130 feet because I felt that breathing Nitrox 32 here was not a good idea for me. I saw Dave make the switch at about 140 feet. He must be taking a big nitrogen narcosis hit. I make the switch at 130 feet. Going from a nitrogen-free air source to a nitrogen rich mix at 130 feet gave me an immediate hit of nitrogen narcosis, which was a bit startling and scary. However, after many dives to the Warren car, I easily adjusted to the nitrogen hit. I hoped Dave was coping as well.

Dave and I spent the next 50 minutes completing our decompression requirements, stopping at the station under the boat with the oxygen regulators. As soon as we surfaced and boarded the boat, Jim and Brett splashed into the lake and began their descent. They surfaced about one 80 minutes later, having completed their assignment. Brett complained that he took a heavy nitrogen narcosis hit when he switched from Heliox to Nitrox 32 at 150 feet.   As the dive boats departed the dive site, anchors were left in place to facilitate the next day's dive operation, to finally recover the bones.

On Monday December 6, the team arrived at the dive locker early, having spent the night before filling staging tanks and mixing new breathing gas. We loaded gear aboard the boats and departed for the dive site. In December, the days start getting shorter and with the high peaks surrounding Lake Crescent, the direct sunlight will only hit the site for 4 or 5 hours. On board was John Rawlings with his assortment of cameras. He wasn't about to miss any of the action. He wanted to join the dive team in the worst way but the National Park Service Dive Program prohibited him from joining the SRC team even as a volunteer.

Brett and Jim dove first. Jim carried two special containers that I had designed to bring the fragile bones to the surface. The two completed their dive in about 90 minutes, surfacing with the two containers now full of Lake Crescent water and the three bones. Dave Conlin and I dove next and picked up all the various travel lines and the down line attached to the Warren car. The Warren family was once again on the shores of the lake at Ambulance Point (Madrona Point) greeting the divers with warm hearts.

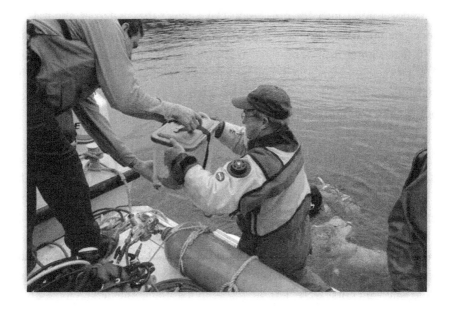

Dr. Dave Conlin is handing the box containing a human skull to Ranger Kevin Hendricks. Courtesy of John Rawlings.

Bone recovery dives in December of 2004. The left photo is of Mike Kalahar handing a tube to Kevin Hendricks. The two femurs were in the tube. In the right photo, Dan Pontbriand is climbing aboard the dive boat after a dive to 200 feet.   Courtesy of John Rawlings.

The special containers were transported to Port Angeles and secured in the park evidence locker for safekeeping. The next task was to identify whose bones these were. The presumption was they were the remains of Russell Warren. The best way to find out was a DNA test. Could DNA be extracted from these old bones submerged in Lake Crescent for 75 years?

Dan Pontbriand on the left with Dr. Dave Conlin returning to the surface. Courtesy of John Rawlings.

14

FULL CIRCLE

The bones were transported to Dr. Katherine Taylor of the King County Medical Examiner's Office on December 17, 2004. We had consulted with her 2 ½ years earlier, asking for her opinion regarding the survivability of bones in fresh water after being submerged for 72 years. It was her professional opinion that the two femur bones, left and right legs, were from the same individual. Both femurs were approximately the same length and exhibited other similar characteristics, suggesting they came from the same person. Based on the length of the femurs, Dr. Taylor estimated the person was between 5 feet 8 inches and 6 feet 2 inches tall. No evidence was found of trauma to either femur. The femurs were heavy enough in material and bone density that she believed it might be possible to extract DNA.

Dr. Taylor also examined the skull and found it to be consistent with the characteristics of a Caucasian male. It consisted of the right and left parietals, occipital and frontal bones. Missing were all of the facial bones including the upper and lower jaw and the inferior part of the cranium. The bones were very soft, chalklike, and fragile, ruling out any radiographic examination.

Mary Lou Rhone Elwood, a third cousin of Rollie Warren, was an accomplished genealogist. She attended the Warren memorial service in July of 2002 at Lake Crescent and was an avid letter writer to her aunt, Louise Allen (whom we met earlier in the book) who lived in Port Angeles. I asked Mary Lou to provide us with a list of living female relatives of Russell. It was easy for her to come up with the information. Russell had a sister named Emily Helen Warren who married John Earl Matteson. Emily and John had a daughter named Jessie Wilma Matteson born on April 10, 1923, in Neillsville, Wisconsin. Emily, had the same Mitochondrial DNA, or mtDNA, (see explanation below) as Russell's mother and therefore the same as Russell. Jessie had the same mtDNA as Emily, therefore Jessie and Russell Warren should have the same Mitochondrial DNA.

The type of DNA that may be easily extracted and sequenced from ancient bones was Mitochondrial DNA (mtDNA). This type of DNA is matrilineal, in other words, it follows the female side of the family. Mothers pass along exact copies of their mtDNA to their daughters who pass it on to their daughters and so on. Males possess their mother's mtDNA but cannot pass it on to their sons

We needed to find Jessie Matteson. Mary Lou provided me with her phone number. Jessie lived in Racine, Wisconsin. I called her and she answered rather quickly. She had already been talking with Mary Lou and had remembered the story of the mysterious disappearance of her relatives, Blanche and Russell Warren, many years ago. She would have been six years old when the Warren's disappeared. I explained to her that we needed a DNA sample from her to help solve the identity of the bones found in Lake Crescent. She would be glad to provide the sample, a simple cheek swab.

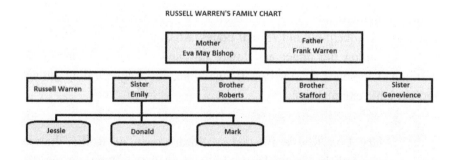

Data courtesy of Mary Lou Elwood

178

In January of 2005, I called the Racine County Medical Examiner's Office and talked to Tom Terry. I told him the whole story, which took a while and explained that we needed a DNA sample from Jessie Wilma Matteson, a resident of Racine. Mr. Terry asked a whole series of questions. I'm sure that initially, he must have thought I was a lunatic from a local tavern, or perhaps a college prank. After a few more questions and answers, however, Mr. Terry finally believed me and took me seriously. It must have been an amazing story to hear for someone who had never heard it before . Mr. Terry was more than happy to help. A letter was drafted to Mr. Terry on official Olympic National Park stationary asking for his assistance.

A few weeks later, Mr. Terry called Jessie Wilma Matteson and explained to her what was going on. She agreed to provide the sample. After acquiring the samples, he carefully packaged them and sent them to Olympic National Park Headquarters. We now had all the biological samples we needed to conduct the DNA examination and comparison. With hopefully, DNA extraction possible from the femurs, we needed to find a lab that performed this kind of exam.

Today, nearly all state crime labs and the FBI forensic lab in Quantico, Virginia, can perform this type of analysis. After Dr. Taylor's examination, the femurs were sent to the FBI laboratory and were received on March 9, 2005. The facility was a busy place with the wars in Iraq, Afghanistan, and various terrorist attacks all over the world. FBI Special Agents were working in many foreign countries assisting with terrorist cases, including DNA analysis. We were honored they would accept our case.

In late January of 2005, I accepted a transfer and left Olympic National Park. I received a significant promotion to the National Park Service Washington DC Headquarters to become the Servicewide Branch Chief of Emergency Services. This highly prized position was fast-paced and high-pressure. One of the functions of this job was as program manager for the Servicewide dive program. I was also the Servicewide Program Manager for Search and Rescue and Emergency

Medical Services programs and later accepted the Servicewide Motorboat Training and Certification program. I must have done something right!

On November 3, 2005, the FBI laboratory completed their report. The mtDNA extracted and sequenced from the bone sample and the mtDNA sample from Jessie Ewing, the grandniece of Russell Warren, were the same. In the words of the FBI lab report, "*Therefore RUSSELL WARREN cannot be excluded as the source of the Q1 (evidence number) bone.*" The bones found in the lake were those of Russell Warren. By early December, nearly every member of the Warren family probably knew that Russell had finally been found. His wife, Blanche, most likely is near his side at the bottom of Lake Crescent, buried in the rocky gravel bottom of the lake.

Russell's bones were turned over to Rollie Warren. They were cremated and the ashes given to his family. In 2009, Jim Warren (Frank Warren's son) and Geneil Warren (Rollie's wife) returned Russell's remains to the shore of Lake Crescent. He now rests in peace near his wife and his son Frank.

The Warren car will remain on the bottom of Lake Crescent, preserved by the deep, cold, dark water.. Only those properly trained and issued a permit by the Park are allowed to make the dive and visit the car.

Visitors coming to Lake Crescent will likely pass the very spot that Blanche and Russell's car left the road in 1929 near Milepost 223. Sheriff Jack Pike, brothers Harry and Ed Brooks, and the rest of Sheriff Pike's investigation team passed away years ago. I hope that somehow, they know that the mysterious case they worked so hard on has been solved.

We owe a great deal of thanks to Sheriff Jack Pike, who left a number of valuable clues for us to find. I hope Frank and Charles Warren are looking down on us. I think they know that their parents loved them very much. Hopefully, they know that we found their father and the 1927 Chevrolet.

Bob Caso still lives in Port Angeles, Washington, and loves to talk about the Warren mystery. He still loves to talk about diving too.

Rollie Warren and his wife, Geneil, live in Idaho. Rollie and Geneil hope to travel often in the years to come. Their daughter, Kristine, her husband and two sons live nearby. Jim Warren (Frank's son) lives in California.

Mary Lou Rhone Elwood lives in Chippewa Falls, Wisconsin, and has retired from a career in nursing.

Jessie Wilma Matteson Ewing passed away in 2007.
Louise Allen passed away in Port Angeles in 2011.

John Rawlings and his wife live in Mill Creek, Washington. He continues to write about diving and underwater photography. Jerome Ryan and his wife live near John Rawlings. Jerome owns an engraving business and has given up diving for the time being to focus on his business.

Bill Walker and his wife, Gwen, live in Arizona. Bill still enjoys diving and loves to talk about it. His son, Joe, and his wife live in Alabama. Joe is an Apache helicopter pilot instructor and is a veteran of Iraq and Afghanistan who still enjoys diving.

Gene and Sandy Ralston live in Idaho and continue to assist families in finding their loved ones underwater when most agencies have given up searching. They continue to hone the fine art of side-scan sonar.

Dan Messaros transferred to Joshua Tree National Park as a District Ranger. He lives there with his wife and daughter.

Barb Maynes still works at Olympic National Park as a Ranger.

Dr. Paul Gleeson retired.

Chief Ranger Curt Sauer retired as Superintendent of Joshua Tree National Park.

Assistant Superintendent Roger Rudolf retired from Olympic National Park.

Ranger Art Sandison still works at Lake Crescent.

Ranger John Ward has retired.

Ranger Larry Lang retired.

Ranger Mike Butler retired.

Ranger Kevin Hendricks transferred to Sequoia and Kings Canyon National Park as the Chief Ranger.

Glen Melville works for another agency.

Paul Seyler and wife and Mike Kalahar and his wife still work at Olympic National Park in the Maintenance Division. Mike still dives with the Olympic National Park dive team.

John Southard and his wife live in Sequim, Washington. John works for a private bio-tech company and is still diving.

Kristin Dizon Anderson and her husband and children live in Seattle. Kristin continues to write and work in the news and media business and raise her family.

Brett Seymour and Dr. Dave Conlin continue to work for the National Park Service Submerged Resources Center out of Denver. Dave was recently promoted to Chief of the Center.

As for me, I retired in November of 2011as the Chief Ranger of Isle Royale National Park. I live in New Hampshire with Marcy. And I love to talk about diving too.

You can get more information about The Missing Ones at our website:

http://www.themissingones.com

Or you can Email me at:

DaniclePontbriand@gmail.com

APPENDIX A

A History of Scuba Diving

It's important to understand the history and perils of scuba diving in order to appreciate the Warren investigation. This case spanned 75 years, from 1929 to 2004, and in that time diving technology made huge advancements.

It all began in 1865, when two French mining engineers, Benoit Rouquayrol and Auguste Denayrouse, designed an underwater breathing device. It consisted of a horizontal steel compressed air cylinder (about 350 PSI) that was carried on the back of a diver, coupled with a valve arrangement, mouthpiece and hose. To take a breath, the diver would have to manually open a valve. The diver was still tethered to the surface, since it was necessary to pump air into the low-pressure tank. The diver could, however, disconnect the hose and swim freely for a few minutes. Divers still did not have a working knowledge of breathing air in water.

In 1933, Yves Le Prieur modified the Rouquayrol-Denayrouse unit by fitting a higher-pressure tank (1500 PSI) to a lower pressure-demand valve on the tank. The diver still needed to open and close a valve to breathe, but the diver was completely free of surface supplied hoses. In 1942 and 1943, the famous French Naval Lieutenant Jacques-Yves Cousteau and engineer Emile Gagnon of Air Liquide (a French natural gas corporation) developed a demand valve regulator unit coupled to a pair of high-pressure compressed-air cylinders. The unit was light and simple. The invention allowed divers to be completely self-contained underwater, free from surfaced supplied air and surface hoses. Divers could swim underwater rather than have to walk on the bottom like the heavy hard hat divers of the time.

In January 1943, Cousteau tested the unit in the Marne River near Paris. After a few more modifications, he patented the Aqua Lung™. The new highly reliable invention revolutionized the underwater world. Later in 1943, Cousteau and two friends (including Frederic Dumas), completed over five hundred dives. Dumas descended, with great planning, to a record depth of 210 feet in the Mediterranean.

The Aqua Lung™ made its U.S. military debut near the end of World War II with the U.S. Navy. The Aqua Lung™ was commercially marketed with great success in France and Great Britain in 1950 and 1951. Aqua Lung™ regulators were available in the U. S. by 1946, and were available on the west coast by 1948.

Self-Contained Underwater Breathing Apparatus, or SCUBA, requires training to master the specialized skills and use the new equipment properly. The Los Angeles County Recreation Department began a comprehensive dive program in 1954. It was not until August of 1955 that the YMCA began offering the first nationally organized course for scuba certification. Prior to this, the only way a sport diver could learn the skill was from a former U.S. Navy diver.

Sport diving has traditionally had a depth limit of 130 feet. About 98 percent of all diving is done in depths shallower than 130 feet. However, there is a growing movement in the modern dive community to expand and improve the type of equipment sport divers can purchase, as well as to develop a skill level that can take divers to much greater depths. These new skills and types of equipment come from the commercial and professional dive industry that has been the testing ground for this development. Many commercial and military divers have been injured and even died as a result of testing new gear and techniques.

The cave diving community has also been a leader in developing new systems and gear. The use of mixed gases such as helium/oxygen/nitrogen and Nitrox has greatly improved dive safety. These gases allow divers to reach much greater depths while giving the diver the ability to have adequate brain function. New decompression charts were developed for the use of these gases.

At sea level, air is composed of about 20.9 percent oxygen, 78 percent nitrogen and the remainder is inert gases such as helium. The air pressure at sea level is about 14.7 pounds per square inch, but this can change slightly in different weather conditions. At 33 feet in fresh water, a diver will feel a pressure of about 29.4 pounds per square inch on his body. First, the diver will feel that pressure on his eardrums as the pressure pushes inward into the ear canal. At 66 feet, the pressure increases to 58.8 pounds per square inch. The deeper a diver descends, the more concentrated amounts of nitrogen (and oxygen) are absorbed into his body. At high pressure, nitrogen suppresses the Central Nervous System, and the diver feels "narced." The diver will experience lightheadedness, tunnel vision, a loss of depth perception, impaired judgment, and, in some cases, anxiety. Jacque Cousteau called it the "rapture of the deep."

As the diver ascends from deep water, the amount of nitrogen absorbed in the blood, is released. It's important the diver ascend slowly and make stops along the way to slowly release this excess nitrogen. Otherwise, bubbles will develop in the blood and accumulate in joints or organs of the body. Think of the bubbles in soda as you open the can or bottle and release the pressure. If divers don't ascend slowly through the water column they could get decompression sickness or the "bends."

APPENDIX B

A History of the SCRU

A Brief History of the National Park Service Underwater

Archaeology Program

The Submerged Cultural Resources Unit (SCRU) was born out a special need for marine archaeology. The specialized dive team stationed in, of all places, Santa Fe, New Mexico, began in 1974, when it's then first diver, Dan Lenihan, was charged with surveying reservoirs for archaeological sites in the western states as dams were built and lakes were formed. An underwater archeologist himself, Park Ranger Lenihan led the first team, with other talented archeologists like Larry Murphy and Toni Carrell. Over time, the SCRU team expanded its tasks to other areas of the country. Many National Park sites had submerged cultural and archaeological resources that were in need of study, inventorying and management. To this day, this team has a remarkable safety program eclipsing similar government programs in wild land and structural fire. Attention to fitness, medical standards, training requirements and dive safety standards is the reason this safety record is to be envied.

Since its inception in 1980, SCRU has been the leader in the federal government in underwater archeology. It has conducted over 120 separate field operations ranging from Alaska to most water parks in the lower 48, to the Virgin Islands, Hawaii and the former Pacific Trust Territories (in Micronesia and Polynesia) and foreign waters including France, Honduras, England, and Mexico. SCRU has provided evidence and expert witnesses to NPS court cases through the Department of Justice (DOJ) in over a dozen separate cases. Unit members have conducted over twenty thousand person-dives in every conceivable condition and supervised approximately forty thousand dives with not a single serious diving accident. Almost every diver in the National Park Service (NPS maintains approximately 150 collateral duty divers) has, at one time or another, been trained by or served in the field with

187

SCRU. The unit was renamed the Submerged Resources Center (SRC) in 2005. The SRC is now stationed in Boulder, Colorado, near the Water Resources Division of the National Park Service. (Written by Butch Farabee)

ABOUT THE AUTHOR

I was born in Maine in 1955 and am the oldest of a set of identical twins. My twin, Edward, is also a National Park Ranger. I attended grade school, high school and college in Maine.

I began working for the National Park Service shortly after I graduated from college in 1979. I worked as a Ranger at Grand Teton National Park, Big Bend National Park, Shenandoah National Park, Boston National Historical Park, Gulf Islands National Seashore and Big Horn Canyon National Recreation Area. I served as a District Ranger at Olympic National Park for fifteen years and then as the Servicewide Chief of Emergency Services at National Park Headquarters in Washington DC (WASO). In December of 2007 I transferred to Sequoia and Kings Canyon National Parks in California and served at the Sequoia District Ranger. Finally, in 2009, I served as Chief Ranger at Isle Royale National Park. I retired in November of 2011 after thirty-one years of service with the National Park Service.

Like most Rangers in the National Park Service system, I started working as a seasonal Ranger. After seven seasons and three National Parks, I decided to apply for permanent jobs, hoping to spend my life working and living in wild places. Some National Park Rangers are tasked with protection duties and are responsible for visitor and resource protection, which can cover a lot of different tasks in one day. I recalled one day about ten years before I retired that summed up what it was like to be a National Park Ranger. I performed a scuba dive in the morning fixing a dock, splinted a fractured leg in the afternoon, arrested a drunk driver in the evening, and fought a wild land fire at night!

Two new books are in the works.

"THE ALGOMA"... A ship wreck off the southern coast of Isle Royale National Park is full of mystery and intrigue. The ALGOMA crashed into Mott Island, part of Isle Royale on November 7th of 1885 in a "Gales of November" storm. The vessel broke apart and took with it 46 lives. It was the largest loss of life of any ship wreck on the Great Lakes, larger even than the Edmond Fitzgerald. Why did the wreck occur and what happened to the passengers and crew? The bow section, where most of the passengers died, reportedly drifted off into deep water and sank. Or did it? Read the story of the captain's tremendous courage to save his crew and the passengers and how the mystery was solved.

"TWIN RANGERS" What is it like to have an identical twin brother who is also a National Park Ranger? We'll share some funny and strange Ranger stories and talk about some unsolved cases that my brother Ed and I worked on.

I hope you enjoyed reading the Second Edition of THE MISSING ONES.

DAN PONTBRIAND

Made in the USA
Middletown, DE
19 April 2024

53126495R00116